RITALIN
IS NOT
THE ANSWER
ACTION GUIDE

RITALIN IS NOT THE ANSWER

ACTION GUIDE

An Interactive Companion
to the Bestselling Drug-Free
ADD/ADHD Parenting Program

David B. Stein, Ph.D.

JOSSEY-BASS
A Wiley Company
San Francisco

Published by

JOSSEY-BASS
A Wiley Company
989 Market Street
San Francisco, CA 94103

www.josseybass.com

Jossey-Bass books and products are available through most bookstores. To contact Jossey-Bass
directly, call (888) 378-2537, fax to (800) 605-2665, or visit our website at www.josseybass.com.

Substantial discounts on bulk quantities of Jossey-Bass books are available to corporations,
professional associations, and other organizations. For details and discount information, contact
the special sales department at Jossey-Bass.

We at Jossey-Bass strive to use the most environmentally sensitive paper stocks available to us.
Our publications are printed on acid-free recycled stock whenever possible, and our paper always
meets or exceeds minimum GPO and EPA requirements.

Library of Congress Cataloging-in-Publication Data
Stein, David B.
 Ritalin is not the answer action guide : an interactive
companion to the bestselling drug-free ADD/ADHD parenting
program / David B. Stein.
    p. cm.
Includes bibliographical references and index.
 ISBN 0-7879-6044-6
 1. Attention-deficit hyperactivity disorder. 2. Behavior
therapy for children. 3. Methylphenidate hydrochloride—Side
effects. 4. Parenting. I. Title.
 RJ506.H9 S682 2002
 616.85'89—dc21   2001007205

FIRST EDITION
PB Printing 10 9 8 7 6 5 4 3 2

CONTENTS

FOREWORD

A nine-year-old, wonderful little boy graduated from therapy with me this week. When he was five he was labeled as ADHD and placed on stimulant medication. Since then several different drugs have been tried. His school work has not improved, and his misbehaviors have become progressively worse. He has only been my patient for the last three months, but in this short time and with the Caregivers' Skills Program (CSP), he is no longer considered an ADHD child. This was accomplished without drugs. At the final session his father said to me:

> I've got my kid back. His spirit is back. He's spontaneous again. He laughs, tells jokes, and plays normally again. During the years he was on all those damn drugs, he lost his humanity. Now he's well behaved, polite, doing well in school, and he's a kid again. I get so angry at the bad advice we were given over the last several years. I feel so sad when I see all those kids at my son's school who take these drugs. They have circles under their eyes, and they seem to have lost their God-given spirit.

I had been searching for the right words to begin this book, and then this father said them for me eloquently. Drugs are a quick and easy fix, but they are unhealthy and they rob us of our humanity.

THE DANGER OF PSYCHOTROPIC DRUGS

I've been teaching psychopharmacology for nearly twenty years, and I've learned a very important lesson: the human body is a miracle. It is very delicately balanced, and drugs, taken over a long period of time, disrupt this normal balance. Very often the changes induced by this disruption are irreversible. I've learned that no drugs should be used unless they are absolutely necessary.

Psychotropic (also known as psychiatric) drugs are very powerful. They are also extremely unhealthy. I am not opposed to the occasional use of these drugs but only for the shortest time periods possible. If a person experiences a tragic loss such as the death of a loved one and becomes profoundly depressed, six months on an antidepressant can help ease the pain. If a person becomes severely anxious about a problem such as the loss of a job, then a short regimen on a tranquilizer may have some benefit. But the long-term use of these drugs to solve our life problems is dangerous business. This is especially important when psychiatric drugs are used in the developing bodies of children. I discuss these health risks in detail in Chapter Two: "The True Facts Parents Are Not Being Told."

Pills mask our problems. When the pills are stopped, the problems are still there, and so is our inability to tackle and cope with the problems. Pills teach us nothing. Pills can rob us of the motivation to solve our problems and our desire to mobilize our personal resources to conquer them. Our humanity—our spirit—is molded when we tackle problems and stresses and overcome them. If we stop doing that, we stop growing. We stop developing spiritually. We stop learning. We stop evolving. We give up our souls.

In the last two years at almost every talk I've given, someone in the audience has said something like this: "I'm a doctor, and I discovered, thanks to a psychologist friend of mine, that I'm ADD. I started taking Adderall [or any other stimulant], and I have a new lease on life. I feel better, and I can think better." My typical response is that probably he could have gotten the same results by using almost any other type of psychiatric drug. An antidepressant may have worked as well, or a tranquilizer, or even whiskey. We are increasingly relying on drugs to help us make it through our difficult days, and when we take drugs to cope, this is called addiction. This person's problem isn't ADD. It's ADD-I-C-T.

THE CHOICES WE CAN MAKE

Drugs are rapidly becoming replacements for self-discipline in our society. But we *have choices* about how to handle our behavioral and emotional problems, which, in our stressed-out society, can be enumerable. If, for example, a man has a long-term problem with depression because he is not happy with his career, he can choose to take antidepressants for years to mask his problem. Or he can choose to see a therapist who may help him develop methods for stress management, perhaps for retraining for a more desirable career and for developing self-discipline techniques to control the thinking patterns that underlie his depression. If a woman has anxiety attacks because her life is filled with unrelenting stresses, she can choose to take tranquilizers for the rest of her life. Or she can change her lifestyle, develop better problem-solving skills, and learn effective cognitive (thinking) coping skills.

My point is that anything drugs can do can also be done in more lasting and healthy ways by learning a variety of psychological techniques for dealing effectively with almost any human problem. But these techniques require dedication, self-discipline, and hard work. Unlike the quick fix and the short-lived gains of pills, however, these changes can be permanent.

The doctor I mentioned earlier who thinks he's ADD and is taking Adderall has choices, too. I sometimes illustrate that by describing my own case. I begin by saying something like this: "Doctor, how do you think I would feel if I had a brain tumor and you just told me you are a neurosurgeon? What kind of confidence would I have in you? Do you think I would decide to use your services? I don't want someone operating on my head who is ADD and needs drugs to focus. I want someone who has self-discipline and who is sensible enough to limit his patient and surgery schedule to a level where he doesn't need pills to help focus and cope."

Then I add: "I'm the proverbial absent-minded professor. My mind is constantly focused on the world of ideas. And this often results in forgetting things, in losing my keys, or in misplacing my glasses. I can take a pill to help. An amphetamine would, indeed, help me calm down and focus better on all these things. Or I can practice being a bit more diligent and making certain I put my keys and glasses in specific locations to help me always know where they are.

I can jot down memos to help jar my memory. One solution requires me to exert self-discipline; the other camouflages my emotions. One is a lasting solution, provided I continue to work at it; the other stops as soon as the pills stop. One maintains my human integrity; the other robs me of it. One helps keep me healthy; the other damages my health. You have the same choice."

TWO POWERFUL FORCES: THE DRUG COMPANIES AND THE PROFESSION OF PSYCHOLOGY

Two forces have been at work to convince the public of their need for drugs to help them cope and to control their children's behavior: (1) the drug companies and (2) the profession of psychology itself. Obviously, the profit motive is huge for drug companies. As for the psychologists—well, I'll get to them later.

The Drug Companies

During the 1990s I observed the pharmaceutical companies waging a successful campaign to market and sell all sorts of psychiatric drugs. Increasingly, they have been able to convince the public that everything is a disease and that the magical solution lies in simply taking a pill. How easy they make it for us! If we are depressed, we have a disease called depression. But don't worry, there is a pill for depression. If we are nervous, we have a disease called anxiety. But don't worry, there is a pill for anxiety. If we have a child who is not behaving well in school and not doing his work properly, he has a disease called attention deficit disorder. But don't worry, we have a pill for ADD, too.

Does it matter whether or not drugs are obtained from the streets or from the doctor's office? Not really. Prescription drugs, just like street drugs, allay nervousness, lift our spirits, and help us cope and make it through stress-filled days. During the 1990s we merely switched pushers. We shifted from the Colombian and Mexican cartels to the pharmaceutical cartels. The law now stalks one and protects the other.

Pharmaceutical companies have been discovering that psychotropic drugs yield enormous profits, often billions of dollars from one drug alone. Some companies have become reliant on these drugs as their largest source of revenue. When they shifted from targeting adults and started targeting the developing bodies of children, my concern changed to fury. They know stimulant drugs are risky. Every textbook I've used for teaching psychopharmacology clearly states what the side effects of these drugs are and that these are the most psychologically addicting drugs known. Surely pharmaceutical executives know this, and yet they have aggressively—and successfully—campaigned to legitimatize these drugs and get as many of our youth hooked on them as possible. And we are now discovering that we can't stop the drugs. When the drugs are stopped, any gains that were made evaporate. Increasingly, we have to keep kids on these drugs into the teenage and adult years. Is this not profitable for the pharmaceutical companies?

The Profession of Psychology

What amazes me most is that my fellow psychologists are supporting the drug companies' campaign. Things have changed vastly in the world of psychology since I trained in psychology in the sixties and seventies. Drugs weren't the basis for treatment then. Excitement and electricity permeated the air because of the excellent research that was being conducted to develop psychological techniques that produced amazing results, especially in child therapy. Lovaas developed techniques that produced miraculous results with autistic children. Paterson and Becker developed excellent parenting programs that produced real results. Bandura developed methods to reduce childhood fears and aggressive behaviors.

When I was training at the University of Mississippi Medical Center in the 1970s, the intern program there was ranked number one in the country for outstanding behavioral research. Behavioral research couldn't be conducted in the major metropolitan areas like New York, Chicago, or Los Angeles because of the entrenched power of the Freudians and Rogerians; neither tradition was research-oriented. But I recently visited with the only remaining professor in my old department; the others are now at universities in larger cities. He said to me frankly that the department is now biologically oriented. I was stunned. I said nothing, but my mind was racing. "What the hell do you mean, biologically oriented? Why aren't you factually oriented? How can a once-great department that produced great works now blindly accept the junk that is being produced? How much grant money is being given to the department and to the hospital to become 'biologically oriented' and to forget its once-great commitment to excellent behavioral treatments?" If being biologically oriented meant that modern research was based on fact and good procedures, then the claim to be biologically oriented would be profound. But such is not the case. I'm sad to say that what is being produced as research today is garbage, and our children are victims because of it.

Psychology seems to have given up on itself. Instead of developing effective cognitive and behavioral methods, psychologists have developed poorly designed behavioral treatments that have been repeatedly demonstrated not to work. The literature is replete with studies indicating that behavioral treatments for attentional disorders don't work, and yet psychologists keep researching and recommending the same old ineffective methods. In order to make any improvements, drugs are now almost always necessary. In fact, the same results are obtained without any psychologically based treatments. Drugs have become the bastion for treating children who misbehave in school and do poor school work. The change in paradigm has shifted from psychological to biological. Why? What has been happening? Why has psychology stopped believing in itself? Why are psychologists no longer carefully examining the poor research and lame methods that are being promulgated as treatments?

I don't know what's happened to the profession of psychology, but I do know this: what I present in the pages of this book works. I believe in psychology. I want my profession to reemerge with zest and aliveness and develop behavioral and cognitive methods that work without poisoning the bodies of children. I receive thousands of letters from parents reporting overwhelming successes without drugs. The CSP is based on accurate and precise behavioral principles.

Lately when I've attended professional conferences, I've been hearing statements supporting the use of stimulant drugs. Here's an example: "The best thing we can do for these children is help them with their self-esteem. By failing in school and constantly getting in trouble with teachers, their self-worth is constantly chipped away. The fastest way to help them is with the proper regimen of medications."

I say that's rubbish! The best way to help children is to teach them the skills and behaviors they need to succeed. Empty improvement with drugs only creates an illusion of meaningful change. What good does it do these children if every time attempts are made to stop the drugs, the improvements disappear? The drugs have not helped them master themselves. Children's humanity lies in controlling their own minds and behaviors. They have to learn self-discipline. School work is hard. The best thing we can do for these children is to help them make real and lasting changes. They can learn to control their behaviors. They can learn to study. They can learn deep concentration. They can learn to memorize. What a horrible thing it is to tell a child he has a disease when not one shred of evidence shows that to be true. Once told, however, a child will most likely believe he is mentally impaired for the rest of his life. When we convince children that they are sick and handicapped and will need pills for the rest of their lives, we rob them of their real sources of self-esteem. We rob them of their ability to learn and conquer. We take away from them the opportunities to dig deep within themselves to discover their personal resources and abilities. We steal from them the meaningfulness of their lives. No, my friends, pills do not give children back their self-esteem. They rob them of it!

I challenge my fellow psychologists to join in the quest. I've clinically tested and researched the program presented in this book. Help me to help children. Research even further the techniques presented here. Improve them. Make them better. Let's get back to believing in psychology and start, once again, producing exciting psychological methods that really work. Let's stop relying on chemicals to do the work for us.

I believe in the contents of this book with a light and uplifted heart. I still believe in psychology. What you learn here works and is healthy for your child. God bless.

DAVID B. STEIN, PH.D.
Professor of Psychology
Longwood College, Farmville, Virginia

To my great and wonderful children,
Alex, Kevin, and Heidi,
with all my love, Dad

To my wonderful friend,
Professor Steve Baldwin,
University of Teeside, UK,
who died tragically March 21, 2001—
one of the great psychologists and thinkers of our time

ACKNOWLEDGMENTS

When I entered the fight to develop effective drug-free treatments for children, I felt very alone. No one was there for support. But the good Lord eventually answered my prayers. Several years ago I met Professor Steve Baldwin from the University of Teeside in Middlebrough, England. Dr. Baldwin was the first to enthusiastically recognize the merit of my work. His encouragement and support sustained me through difficult times. He was one of the most gifted psychologists I've ever known. His knowledge was vast, and I came to rely on his opinions. We collaborated on several exciting projects. He succeeded in getting the British government to support a drug-free treatment clinic, using the Caregivers' Skills Program. The clinic's doors opened in November 2000. In March of 2001, he called to report that the initial test cases were proving successful, and we talked for hours about making things even better. During the week of that conversation, Steve was killed in a train accident. His students, Emmi Froeme and Becky Anderson, desperately tried to reach me ahead of the news media. What wonderful and thoughtful young people they are. The university's administrators have been thoughtful and considerate in maintaining contact with me. I grieve Steve's death. I will endeavor to maintain, in his honor, the standards and integrity of research for which he stood. God be with you my friend.

I'm deeply indebted to pediatrician Dr. DuBose Ravenel. He is one of the most amazing physicians I have ever met. His dedication to the children under his care is awesome. Affectionately known as Dr. Bose, he is devoted to finding treatments that not only produce improvements but are healthiest for the children. He is a clear and objective thinker who takes great pains to avoid accepting the junk research presently being foisted on his and my profession and to carefully scrutinize every piece of research that comes out. Often he is the first to call me to say, "Dave, you've got to take a look at this study. You won't believe your eyes."

Dr. Bose was one of the first practicing physicians to take an interest in my work. One day a few years ago I received a phone call from him requesting more information to help with the care of his patients. That call began a new and wonderful friendship—one that I deeply believe was guided by the hand of the good Lord. Bose and I are now close friends. His insights and comments help keep me on track. I've come to trust his judgment and frequently rely on his input. Much of the improvement made in this and my other works come from suggestions made by Dr. Bose.

Another blessing has come my way. Almost two years ago, I started corresponding with John Rosemond through an introduction made by Dr. Ravenel. John has three great qualities I very much admire. He is a clear thinker, he has great integrity, and he has great courage. It is fashionable to accept the massive amounts of junk and the unethical child diagnosis and treatment literature presently being produced by the psychological and psychiatric communities. John has stood alone for many years to raise public consciousness about the psychobabble that is being preached. He reaches millions of readers, and often he has taken considerable flack for his honest and accurate commentaries, but he has never wavered. His advice to readers is excellent—first rate, in fact. Millions of children have benefited from his books, his speeches, and his syndicated newspaper parenting advice column. His support is personally very meaningful to me because I respect his judgment and his opinions; there are few individuals about whom I can say this. I am proud to now be a member of John's Affirmative Parenting Team and, most important, to have him as a friend.

I am deeply indebted to all my friends and colleagues in the International Center for the Study of Psychology and Psychiatry. I've met some fabulous people; for their support, advice, and help I'm deeply grateful. My love and thanks to Dr. Peter Breggin, Ginger Breggin, Sue Parry, Dr. Nora Porter, Dr. Kevin Mcready, Dr. Ty Colbert, Dr. Jay Joseph, Dr. David Cohen, Dr. Dominic Riccio, Dr. Lloyd Ross, Dorothy Cassidy, Dr. Brian Kean, Dr. Fred Baughman, Adina Lambert, and all the tireless professionals devoted to the well-being of our children.

I'm deeply grateful to my colleague at Longwood College, Dr. Carolyn Craft. What an exceptional person she is. She is an outstanding scholar, and she is unwavering in her dedication to quality teaching. She is, for me, a model in courage. She expects the best from her students and does not settle for less. They are blessed to have her as their professor. Dr. Craft has devoted many hours from her overwhelming schedule to edit my manuscripts. Her support and advice are invaluable, and I treasure her friendship. She has helped me weather several spiritual storms.

Joyce Trent, secretary for the Department of Psychology, devoted countless hours to the typing and editing of my manuscripts. Her honesty and forthrightness are invaluable. If what I wrote was lousy, she said so. To me that is the hallmark of a true friend.

My assistant, Lucinda Whitehead, has helped keep my life in order. My writings have generated about a thousand e-mails and letters weekly from concerned parents, teachers, psychologists, psychiatrists, and other mental health professionals. I couldn't hope to keep up with these correspondences, my writings, and my teaching responsibilities were it not for Lucinda. Thank you, thank you, thank you. Lucinda is also helping with a very intense and in-depth research project that is consuming much of her time. Again, thank you.

My thanks to Alan Rinzler at Jossey-Bass Publishers for his support. He was the first to recognize and believe in my work.

And finally, the friendship of Laura Birdsong, Barry Kudlowitz, Ira Rakoff, and Lois Rakoff has sustained me over many years and through many difficult times.

DAVID B. STEIN

INTRODUCTION:
IS THIS BOOK FOR YOU?

Are you a parent who is reading this opening paragraph because you are concerned about your child? I'll bet most of you are. So place a check mark next to those statements that apply to your situation:

❑ Your child is not doing well in school.

❑ Your child usually brings home report cards with poor grades.

❑ Your child, according to the teacher, might have an attention deficit disorder.

❑ The teacher said your child can't seem to pay attention in class.

❑ The teacher said your child often daydreams during the school day.

❑ Your child's teacher has repeatedly told you that your son or daughter talks constantly during class.

❑ The teacher has told you many times that your child cannot seem to sit still.

❑ The teacher has told you countless times that your son or daughter frequently disrupts the class.

❑ You often receive disturbing notes from the teacher saying that your child rudely calls out answers that are often incorrect.

❑ You frequently receive notes that your son or daughter pushes other children when in line.

❑ At home your child seems like a tightly wound spring and is constantly on the go.

❑ It is extremely difficult to control your child at home.

❑ Your child behaves badly when you go out in public, such as to the grocery store or to church, the synagogue, or the mosque.

❑ Your nerves are shot, and you feel guilty because there are times when you intensely dislike like your son or daughter.

❑ The school guidance counselor contacted you and recommended that your child be tested for attention deficit disorder (ADD) or attention deficit hyperactive disorder (ADHD).

❑ You do not want your child taking drugs to control his or her behavior or attention problems.

If you answered yes to most or many of these questions—most important, yes to the last question—then cheer up. This book, along with its companion book, *Ritalin Is Not the Answer: A Drug-Free, Practical Program for Children Diagnosed with ADD or ADHD*, will teach you how to make all these problems disappear.

In this workbook you will learn how to work with your child using the Caregivers' Skills Program (CSP). You'll find out how to help your child improve his grades, behave well in his classes, and be well behaved at home and in public without the use of any mood-altering drugs. The four chapters in Part One prepare you for the six steps of the CSP; these are described in Part Two. Part Three adds crucial information that will help you maintain all the gains you make with your child.

You will see dramatic improvements within two weeks of beginning the CSP. But most important, you will soon be able to say, "He seems so much happier."

The changes that take place during this journey will never disappear—*as long as you continue to use the skills you will be learning.* If you stop actively working with your child, all improvements will evaporate. You will be learning powerful parenting skills, not receiving the benefits of a miracle. Your dedication and continuing application of these skills are essential for this program to work. If you are motivated and do not want your child on drugs, read on.

RITALIN
IS NOT
THE ANSWER

ACTION GUIDE

Part One

PREPARATION FOR THE CAREGIVERS' SKILLS PROGRAM

I

QUESTIONS
TO ASK
THE DOCTOR

You may have read several books about ADD or ADHD and as a result are thoroughly confused. As a parent you want to do everything possible to help your child. Along comes Dr. Stein, and you're now reading new things that differ from most of what you have read before. Whom should you believe? To help with your decision I've created a lighthearted one-act play. Recognizing how burdened your heart may be at this moment, I've written this little play in a tongue-in-cheek, comedic fashion that I hope will ease your discomfort. I am fully aware of the seriousness of the issues.

The play is written to expose the folly of currently popular beliefs and to show how little the professional community knows about the issues. It assumes that many of you are at the stage where your child has the problems listed in the Introduction section, and you have been advised by your teachers or guidance counselors at schools to undergo a battery of tests to determine whether your child has ADD or ADHD.

Before beginning our play, please complete these homework assignments:

- *For the parent(s):* You are required to ask your doctor all the questions our fictitious parents ask of their doctor performing the evaluation. Take this book with you when you make your own visit, and make certain you don't miss any questions. To help, check the boxes provided alongside each question. On the lines provided just below our hypothetical doctor's answers, write the answers given by the psychologist who tests your child. Compare your recorded answers with the ones given by our play's doctor. I believe you will have two reactions: (1) you will be amazed by the similarities between our imaginary doctor's answers and your recorded ones, and (2) you will be surprised by how much the answers reveal about how little the professionals truly know about ADD and ADHD.

- *For the psychologists, other mental health professionals, educators, and physicians who are reading this book:* You are required to be open-minded and to carefully explore your hearts and minds about what you thought you knew and what you are doing to our children. You are required to be brutally honest with yourselves. I'm on your side; I am not the enemy. My wish is to help you clarify critical issues and point you in the direction of more healthy treatment alternatives.

YOUR KID IS SICK

(A One-Act Play)

Scene: The psychologist's office.

Cast: Mr. Ed Ipal Socrates and his lovely wife, Electra

The psychologist, Dr. Noah Lott

The doctor enters with a serious look on his face. He is carrying a package of official-looking documents.

DOCTOR

Well, Mr. and Mrs. Socrates, it's good to see you. I have the results of your son Rex's tests.

Mr. and Mrs. Socrates squirm nervously.

It appears that Rex has ADHD. That's attention deficit hyperactivity disorder.

Mrs. Socrates begins to cry, pulls out a handkerchief, and blows her nose. She turns to her husband.

MRS. SOCRATES

I knew it. It's been in your family for years. None of you can ever remember anything. All you and your family do is ask questions, over and over again. You never get anything right the first time. You never even pay attention to me.

(Parent-reader: pay attention, check the boxes on the left for the questions to ask your doctor. Record your doctor's answers on the lines below Dr. Noah Lott's answers.)

MR. SOCRATES

❑ Doctor, what do you mean, Rex has ADHD?

DOCTOR

It means that your son has a neurobiological disorder—a disease of his brain and nervous system that prevents him from paying attention and from being able to control his behavior.

_____

_____

_____

Mrs. Socrates cries louder.

MR. SOCRATES

❑ Oh my. Well doctor, where exactly is this disease?

DOCTOR

Well, we're not certain. Research shows that it could be a chemical imbalance or a defect in his brain's metabolism or a problem with some of the anatomy or parts of his brain.

_____

_____

_____

MR. SOCRATES

❑ Oh goodness, doctor. Which of the tests that you gave Rex indicate that he has this disease?

DOCTOR

Actually, you see, none of the tests show that he has a disease.

_____

_____

_____

MR. SOCRATES

❏ Well, which of the tests indicate that he has ADHD?

DOCTOR

Actually, there is no test for ADHD.

_____

_____

_____

Mr. Socrates glares at Dr. Noah Lott.

MR. SOCRATES

❏ Well, what tests did all those researchers do to find all of these ADD and ADHD diseases?

DOCTOR

They found these diseases using other, different tests: CAT scans, MRIs, EEGs, PET scans, and blood tests.

_____

_____

_____

MR. SOCRATES

❏ Good. Now we're getting somewhere. When can we schedule Rex for one of those tests?

DOCTOR

Well, we can't. There are no such tests available for office or hospital testing.

_____

_____

_____

MR. SOCRATES

❑ Are you telling me that all those researchers have made claims of discovering the things that cause these diseases called ADD and ADHD but that none of these tests are good enough to test my son here in the real world? Are you telling me that you can't repeat these tests to confirm my son's diagnosis?

DOCTOR

Well, yes, we can't repeat these tests.

_____

_____

_____

MR. SOCRATES

You sure do say "well" a lot.

DOCTOR

Well, I guess so.

_____

_____

_____

MR. SOCRATES

❑ What tests did you give my son to make this ADD-ADHD diagnosis?

DOCTOR

The doctor takes out his handkerchief and begins wiping his brow. His hands are beginning to tremble slightly.

DOCTOR

The battery of tests included an intelligence test, some tests for his reading, writing, and math skills, some personality tests, and the questionnaire that you filled out.

_____

_____

_____

MR. SOCRATES

❑ Well, which of those tests show that he has ADHD?

Dr. Noah Lott starts to sweat profusely. His voice becomes soft and meek.

DOCTOR

The questionnaire that you filled out.

_____

_____

_____

MRS. SOCRATES

❑ Doctor, how much are you charging for this battery of tests?

DOCTOR

One thousand dollars.

_____

_____

_____

MR. SOCRATES

❑ Are you telling us that your entire diagnosis is based on that questionnaire?
❑ What the hell were all those other tests for?

DOCTOR

Yes, to your first question. And, uh, well, the other tests were given to measure Rex's overall intelligence, to rule out any learning problems, and to make certain he has no comorbid diseases.

_____

_____

_____

MR. SOCRATES

❑ We already know the child is intelligent. He can read the instructions to fix things better and faster than I can, and he reads the sports section in the newspaper every day. He can name every player on every baseball team in the country. He plays video games like a pro for hours. He beats me all the time. How can he do all that and be ADHD?

Dr. Noah Lott appears to be becoming more and more agitated. He starts to stutter.

DOCTOR

Well, you see, uh, well, ADHD is a selective disease. It doesn't manifest itself when a child does tasks that he likes or that are immediately reinforcing, but it seems to appear when a child does tasks he doesn't like or that aren't immediately reinforcing.

_____

_____

_____

MR. SOCRATES

❑ Hell doctor, I do that myself, all the time in fact, and I'm a professor of philosophy. Do I have ADHD too?

DOCTOR

Well, it is genetic. It does run in families.

_____

_____

_____

MRS. SOCRATES

There you go, doctor. That's the first thing you said today that makes any sense to me. My Edgar here is a bit of a featherhead, and so's his whole family. Edgar doesn't pay much attention to me, you know. Isn't that a sign of an attention deficit disorder? Can you fix that doctor?

MR. SOCRATES

❑ Please don't call me Edgar, honey. You know I hate that name. Doctor, you said you were testing to see if my son has any comorbid diseases? How could he have comorbid diseases if you can't tell he has the first disease?

DOCTOR

Now, now Mr. Socrates, let's not get snippy. I gave your son two personality tests, the House-Tree-Person test and the Rorschach Inkblot test, and they indicate that Rex has depression and oppositional-defiant disorder.

_____

_____

_____

MR. SOCRATES

❑ When I minored in psychology in college, I was taught that these types of tests are not valid. I was told that they are inaccurate and that they cannot predict behavior of any kind. Is that true?

_____

_____

_____

DOCTOR

Well, yes that's true. But the tests help get an overall picture of things.

_____

_____

_____

MR. SOCRATES

❏ Of what use are any of these tests if none of them are accurate?

DOCTOR

Well, the intelligence test is accurate. I never thought about that. It's what I was trained to do, and it's what the literature tells us to do.

_____

_____

_____

MR. SOCRATES

❏ OK doc, you got me for a thousand bucks. Now tell me what are we going to do about my son?

DOCTOR

We find that a combination of treatment approaches works best for children with ADD or ADHD. I'll teach you a behavioral program called a token economy program and a few other behavior modification techniques to help you work with your son. I'll also refer you to Dr. Notso Sober, a psychiatrist, for medication.

_____

_____

_____

MR. SOCRATES

❏ How well do these behavior modification treatments work?

DOCTOR

They really don't work well at all. They usually don't work without the medication.

_____

_____

_____

MR. SOCRATES

❑ Then why are you recommending them?

DOCTOR

It's what I've been trained to do, and it's what the literature says to do.

_____

_____

_____

MR. SOCRATES

❑ Does the medication work?

DOCTOR

Yes, indeed. Works about the same whether or not you use the behavioral methods. In fact, we really don't need the behavioral methods.

_____

_____

_____

MR. SOCRATES

❑ You just put my mind at ease. For a while there I couldn't make up my mind if you were dishonest or just plain ignorant, and I just ruled out dishonest. Now, dare I ask about these medications? What are they?

DOCTOR

Well, there are several different drugs; they are all related to the family of drugs known as amphetamines.

_____

_____

_____

MRS. SOCRATES

What?! You want to put my son on amphetamines?

MR. SOCRATES

❑ Now calm down, honey. What do these drugs do?

DOCTOR

They restore the chemical imbalance.

_____

_____

_____

MR. SOCRATES

❑ They restore a chemical imbalance that you don't even know is off balance to begin with?

DOCTOR

Yes. No. No. . . . I . . . think so. You're confusing me!

_____

_____

_____

MR. SOCRATES

❑ I've read in the papers that these drugs are listed as controlled substances because they are habit forming or potentially addictive.

DOCTOR

Well, yes. But lots of research says they're safe.

_____

_____

_____

MR. SOCRATES

❑ Who funds this research?

DOCTOR

The pharmaceutical companies.

_____

_____

_____

MR. SOCRATES

❏ Do you think that might constitute a wee bit of a conflict of interest?

DOCTOR

They do the same thing for all other types of drugs.

_____

_____

_____

MR. SOCRATES

❏ As far as I know, don't other types of drugs work on clearly identifiable diseases? Today have we not been talking about some imaginary diseases that no one can clearly seem to find?

DOCTOR

There are diseases where we can't find the causes, such as headaches, back pain, and joint pain.

_____

_____

_____

MR. SOCRATES

❏ Aren't these people in pain, and doesn't that indicate something is wrong with their bodies? These ADHD kids ain't in pain. Their parents are! Maybe it's the parents that have the disease?

DOCTOR

I never thought of it that way. Actually, I recently discovered that I have ADD, and I started on Adderall, and I've been feeling much better. It calms me down and helps me deal better with people like you.

_____

_____

_____

MR. SOCRATES

❑ Aren't these drugs habit forming or addicting?

DOCTOR

Well, they can be but not if they are taken in the prescribed way.

_____

_____

_____

MR. SOCRATES

❑ Don't we have a youth and teen drug culture out there? Aren't kids grinding Ritalin up and snorting it? How can you tell which kids will always take these drugs in the prescribed way? And why are kids snorting it if it's so safe?

DOCTOR

Well, the literature says these drugs are safe. We can't tell which child might abuse these drugs. We don't have any psychological or medical tests to tell us which kids might abuse drugs or become addicted. So some kids snort it because it acts just like cocaine.

_____

_____

_____

MR. SOCRATES

❑ Who funded this research that says these drugs are safe?

DOCTOR

Well, the pharmaceutical companies.

_____

_____

_____

MR. SOCRATES

❑ Did you know that when he was a young man, Sigmund Freud used cocaine to help with his hectic schedule? Made him feel better too for a while, but then he realized it was no good for him. Why don't you try cocaine?

DOCTOR

What a splendid suggestion. It's important to feel good, you know.

_____

_____

_____

MR. SOCRATES

❑ What's Adderall? And why didn't you take Ritalin?

DOCTOR

I tried Ritalin, and it didn't work for me. But Adderall makes me feel real good. It has a combination of two amphetamines in it, you know—Benzedrine and Dexedrine.

_____

_____

_____

MR. SOCRATES

❑ Maybe your diagnosis isn't ADD; maybe it's A-D-D-I-C-T! Seems to me that you're taking a pill to make you feel better in order to make it through a tough day. Would it be OK if I used whiskey to make it through the day? Whiskey isn't even considered a controlled substance, and I don't even need a prescription. Would it be OK for you to stay high on your Adderall, and I can stay high on whiskey? We can give my son Ritalin, and then the three of us can have a party. What's the difference which drug we take?

DOCTOR

Well, I never thought of it that way.

_____

_____

_____

MR. SOCRATES

❑ Are there any other bad things we need to know about these drugs?

DOCTOR

Well, they stunt children's growth while they're on the drugs. But they catch up when the drugs are stopped. I think. Some kids get some real nasty side effects like stomach problems, blood pressure and heart problems, sleep problems, depression. And they may even act crazy.

_____

_____

_____

MR. SOCRATES

❑ I'm beginning to figure out who's crazy here! Will these drugs help my child's grades improve?

DOCTOR

Only for a short while, and then the grades usually start going down again. Actually, the drugs only help with simple tasks like adding two plus two, but they interfere with learning more complex things like understanding poetry or deciphering a short story. Mostly they keep a child high and make him sit still.

_____

_____

_____

MR. SOCRATES

❑ Let me sum up what we've gotten for our money. You tell me my son has a disease called ADHD, but none of the tests you gave can actually tell us that he has this disease. There are no medical tests and no psychological tests for it! But you tell us parents that our child has a disease? Then you tell us that you don't have any psychological treatments that really work, so we should put him on amphetamines, which can be potentially addicting and harmful to his health—*and* which don't really help him with his learning but only zone him out, make him sit still. Tell me something, doctor, is there something about taking a degree in psychology that makes people like you lose all common sense?

DOCTOR

Well, it's what I've been trained to do and what the literature says to do.

_____

_____

_____

MRS. SOCRATES

I'm truly glad we met you doctor. We'll pray for you.

_____

This draws our little play to an end. What have you learned? I ask this ques-tion of both parents and professionals. What have you learned?

2

THE TRUE FACTS PARENTS ARE NOT BEING TOLD

In 1970 a law was passed called the Federal Drug Control Act, which was aimed at the rampant abuse of several drugs such as heroin, cocaine, amphetamines, and prescription sedatives and tranquilizers. The passage of this law ended a period of twenty years known as the doctor feel-good era (Witters, Venturelli, and Hanson, 1992). Part of the problem preceding the drafting of this law was that physicians were too freely writing prescriptions for mood-altering, psychiatric drugs to heal even the most minor complaints such as the anxiety and fatigue associated with long work hours. The occasional use of powerful drugs quickly changed to abuse, excessive use, and even addiction. The government had become concerned that things had gotten very much out of hand. To bring the situation under control the Comprehensive Drug Abuse, Prevention and Control Act, also known as the Controlled Substances Act (CSA), was passed in 1970.

At the time two categories of drugs were of most concern: the narcotic drugs and the amphetamines. The new law was primarily aimed at controlling the abuse of drugs in these two categories. The act controlled how physicians were permitted to prescribe mind-altering drugs.

Drugs were divided into schedules, numbering I through V. Schedule I drugs were considered too risky for abuse and addiction and were therefore not permitted for prescribing; included were heroin and LSD. Schedule II drugs were the highest level of potentially addictive and abused drugs that doctors were permitted to prescribe. Prescription writing was carefully controlled; the doctor could not order refills without writing a new prescription or calling in a new prescription every ninety days. The schedules were as follows:

- *Schedule I:* No prescriptions are allowed; addiction and abuse potential are high; examples are heroin, quaalude, LSD, hallucinogens, marijuana.

- *Schedule II:* Prescription writing is controlled; addiction and abuse potential is high; examples are opium, morphine, Ritalin, amphetamines, cocaine.

- *Schedule III:* These drugs have less potential for abuse and addiction.

- *Schedule IV:* These drugs have low abuse and addiction potential.

- *Schedule V:* The category includes all over-the-counter drugs.

It is worth noting that if an individual is caught possessing a Schedule II drug without a prescription, he faces potential imprisonment for life and a fine that could range from $2 to $8 million. Ritalin, as an amphetamine-like drug, is classified in Schedule II. This is what we're putting our kids on so casually.

A BRIEF HISTORY OF STIMULANT DRUGS

Very careful consideration was given to the categorization of these drugs. It was not by accident that the amphetamines were classified in Schedule II. During World War II and the Korean War, amphetamines were issued to soldiers to calm them down before combat and to help them stay awake and alert (Witters, 1992). At the end of each war it appeared that abuse was massive; many returning soldiers felt the compulsion to keep using these drugs, which precipitated addiction problems. Because money was made available to veterans for college expenses, amphetamines appeared as drugs of abuse on college campuses. Benzedrine and Dexedrine, called Bennies and Dexies, were among the most popular.

Thus the law was passed in 1970, and the abuse problem was brought under control fairly well. One would think we had learned our lessons about these drugs. Apparently not.

Targeting Our Children

Our children are now the targets for drug use. And now that the drugs are plentiful, they are once again being abused. But this time abuse is not by adults but by children and teenagers. Please note that Benzedrine may not be prescribed by itself to either children or adults, yet it is combined with Dexedrine in Adderall—a drug increasingly being prescribed for children.

What have we done? How have doctors, educators, and parents been convinced that these drugs are innocuous and safe? I've been teaching psychopharmacology for almost twenty years, and every textbook I've used introduces amphetamines as being among the most addictive and abused drugs known. When the term *addictive* is used, it usually does not refer to physical addiction. This is, indeed, a severe problem for some drugs, such as the opiate-related drugs, but psychological addiction is of most concern. Psychological addiction is far more responsible for getting people hooked on drugs than physical addiction.

Two basic properties underlie psychological addiction. Drugs (1) produce a sense of euphoria, commonly referred to as a high, and (2) reduce anxiety and sadness or provide an escape from stress. Amphetamines do both, and they have one additional property: they make people feel energetic and alert.

The Myth of the Paradoxical Effect

Gordon Alles (cited in Witters, Venturelli, and Hanson, 1992), the pharmacology researcher who developed Benzedrine, reported that it helped him with his breathing difficulty while reducing his fatigue, increasing his alertness, and *making him feel euphoric*.

At one time it was believed that this combined alertness and calm occurred only in children who were classified by the old term *hyperkinetic*, now known as ADD-ADHD. This became known as a paradoxical effect. This myth, begun in 1937 by Dr. Charles Bradley, has been completely refuted. These effects—feeling both calm and alert (and euphoric or stoned)—can occur in anyone, and that is precisely the problem. These properties may cause any child or any adult to become addicted.

We professionals in psychology and psychiatry have no way of telling which child may become addicted. There is no medical or psychological test to serve as a warning sign. To make matters worse, we have a dismal track record for successfully treating addictions once they've been triggered (Peele, 1995). These drugs can trigger an addiction in children; once they are launched, we are almost completely powerless to help them.

Sometimes when I give presentations, a physician in the audience will raise his hand and state that he has been prescribing these drugs for a long time with no reports of abuse or addiction. I think these claims are sincere. I see things very differently, however. I see physicians' offices that are so busy that doctors don't connect with the emotional or psychological problems of their patients, much less with children who would be terrified to openly make such a confession. How can there be so many reports of Ritalin abuse in middle schools, high schools, and colleges, yet doctors aren't seeing it in their practices? The truth is, these doctors haven't a clue as to what's really going on with many of their young patients.

In my psychopharmacology course I teach the physical warning signs of alcohol abuse. I've had many patients with alcohol problems tell me that their physician noticed these signs but immediately backed off with no further investigation when the patient said he only "drank two beers a day." Many physicians are not trained to probe for emotional or psychological problems, so it doesn't surprise me that they have been missing the emerging abuse problem with Ritalin. Sadly, it won't be long before young people discover that they can use any of the amphetamines to get high on. Which child, once initiated, will find it easy to stop using?

In frank discussions with my college students I've asked if Ritalin is really being snorted like cocaine and if it produces a high? I guess because they feel comfortable with me, they readily report that yes, it is used commonly at parties, and yes, it produces quite a buzz—one that lasts for a very long time. Reflect, if you will, on the fact that the pharmacological action of Ritalin in the body is almost completely identical to that of cocaine (DeGrandpre, 1999).

A True Story: Kyle

In Chapter One of *Ritalin Is Not the Answer* I discussed the case of Kyle Jones. I had been treating his mother for depression because Kyle had become addicted to heroin and was in jail for selling drugs to support his habit. He had been started on Ritalin when he was ten years old. Mrs. Jones, against her protests, had been bullied by the school psychologist, the school administrators, and his teachers into administering Ritalin to Kyle. Once started, he couldn't stop, and he progressed to other drugs. At the time I wrote the book, Kyle was serving his five-year jail term.

More has happened during the intervening years. Mrs. Jones completed her treatment, and I had not heard from her for a couple of years. She called about a year ago to tell me that Kyle was dead. After completing his five-year term and immediately after being released, Kyle resumed his drug habit. Within a month, he died from an overdose.

Did Kyle have a predisposition for addiction? Apparently, yes. Did Ritalin trigger his addiction? Both Mrs. Jones and I believe that it did. Could this have been avoided? We have no way of knowing. Maybe, if Kyle had never been started on emotion- and mind-altering drugs, his addiction could have been avoided. But the system did start him, and his addiction did result. How many more Kyles are out there? We're playing Russian roulette with those children's lives.

OTHER RISKS OF STIMULANTS

These drugs present other risks. They have short-term side effects such as high blood pressure, heart arrhythmia, stomach irritability, mood changes, agitation and restlessness, tics, lethargy and drowsiness, loss of appetite, loss of weight, nausea, and abdominal pains (*Physician's Desk Reference*, 2000; Breggin, 1998; Maxmen and Ward, 1993).

Growth and Development Suppression

The most alarming side effect is known as growth suppression (Swanson and others, 1993). This means that these drugs, any of them, slow down or even completely stop the production of growth hormone and, in turn, the growth of all parts of a child's body, including head size, brain size, and height. Parents are told not to worry because their child will catch up when the drugs are stopped. Weiner (1982) has pointed out that we have no way of knowing how big or how tall a child would have become if he had never taken the drugs.

These drugs interfere with normal growth during years when crucial developmental events are unfolding (Breggin, 1998), such as the development of neural pathways, the establishment of receptor sites on neurons, development of secondary sexual characteristics, and the overall development of a normal body, which usually unfolds on nature's timetable. When considering this growth-suppression problem, it is important to note that children are supposed to catch up when they stop taking the drug, but there is a growing tendency to keep these children on the drugs for an increasing number of years. When attempts are made to stop them, any behavioral improvements disappear. No child can learn how to behave from a drug. What will additional years of being on these drugs do to children's brains and bodies? No one knows.

Cognitive Toxicity

One other notable side effect is called cognitive toxicity (Swanson and others, 1993); the drugs improve learning for the simpler skills like addition or subtraction but impair more complex cognitive skills like understanding a scientific concept, understanding a poem, or writing a meaningful essay. This phenomenon occurs in 40 percent of children taking the drug.

There are no long-term studies of what these drugs may do to a child's body and nervous system ten or twenty years later.

THE RITALIN LITIGATION CONFERENCE 2001

How have Ritalin and the amphetamines once again become legitimate since the passage of the CSA? I've examined the so-called research touting these drugs as safe, and I notice the names of a dozen or so researchers appearing over and over again.

Recently I attended the Ritalin Litigation Conference in New York—a conference of attorneys and doctors who are involved in legal actions against the pharmaceutical companies manufacturing the various drugs used for ADD and ADHD children; both sides were represented.

The law firms that prevailed against the tobacco industry are now targeting the pharmaceutical companies. Richard Scruggs, one of the leading plaintiff attorneys, stated at the conference that the lawyers are not in this fight for the money; they have more than enough. They are in this because they believe that a handful of pharmaceutical company executives, along with a handful of unscrupulous researchers, have used science to orchestrate the acceptance and popularization of these drugs. Scruggs further stated that as more and more documentation becomes available, he becomes increasingly convinced of the reprehensible conduct of these executives and researchers and that he and the other lawyers will not go away. They will hold all who are responsible to be accountable for their conduct.

I think the next five to seven years will prove very interesting. I personally cannot say who bothers me more, the individuals who have orchestrated this ugly show or the far greater number of sheep who have blindly accepted what has been sold.

THE DISEASE ISSUE

Whether or not ADD and ADHD are diseases is closely intertwined with the drug issue. Mainstream medicine predominantly uses medicines to treat diseases. In American culture, there is an almost automatic association between disease and medicine. If psychiatric disorders can be conceptualized as diseases, the stage is set for the logical treatments: medicines. In order to justify the use of amphetamines, a massive campaign has been under way to convince the American professional community and the public that ADD and ADHD are diseases.

It appears that the strategy to win this argument is to replace qualitative scientific research with an overwhelming volume, or quantity, of lame and poor-quality research. Richard DeGrandpre (1999), a psychopharmacologist, calls this junk science; I call it unethical science (Stein and Baldwin, 2000). Hundreds of studies have appeared in psychiatric and psychological journals claiming to have discovered the underlying brain, nervous system, anatomical, physiological, or bodily abnormality that causes children to not pay attention, mostly in school, and to misbehave.

ADD-ADHD Disease Theories

Examine the list that follows to get a small idea of the various parts of the brain and body that are bring implicated as the causes of ADD and ADHD.

Area of the Brain or Chemical Imbalance Implicated	Author and Date of Study
Brain stem	Lahat and others, 1995
Caudate nucleus	Castellanos and others, 1994
Corpus callosum	Giedd and others, 1994
Dopamine	Levy, 1991
Folic acid	Greenblatt, Huffman, and Reiss, 1994
Frontal lobe	Heilman, Voeller, and Nadeau, 1991
Brain metabolism	Zametkin and others, 1993
Prefrontal cortex	Amen, Paldi, and Thisted, 1993
Serum lipid	Arnold, Kleykamp, Votolato, and Gibson, 1994
Serotonin	Halperin and others, 1997

Not one of these nor hundreds of other studies has gained acceptance in the scientific community. And yet, curiously, the idea or perception that ADD and ADHD are diseases has become commonplace. If this seems like a paradox to you, you're correct. It is. Look what has happened to our common use of language: "My child has ADHD" or "My child was diagnosed with ADHD." So automatic is the use of this language that even I did not notice an error in the title of my previous book. See if you can spot it: *Ritalin Is Not the Answer: A Drug-Free, Practical Program for Children Diagnosed with ADD or ADHD.* Did you pick up on the word *with?* The title should have read . . . *Diagnosed as ADD or ADHD.*

The Pharmacological Industrial Complex

Almost all of this type of research is funded by one of two sources: the pharmaceutical companies or the National Institutes of Mental Health (NIMH), which has been pro disease and pro drug for many years (Breggin, 1998; Valenstein, 1998). Elliot Valenstein presents a profound, scholarly argument about how these two funding sources have contaminated psychiatric and psychological research. He highlights the pressure exerted on university and medical professors to produce large amounts of research for pay raises and promotions and how they are also pressured to obtain money for research grants; the pharmaceutical company grants are the easiest to get. And woe to the professor who produces findings that discredit the desires of the company executives.

Valenstein also points out other concerns, such as editors of psychiatric journals being appointed to pharmaceutical company board positions and researchers' trips to conventions (often in exotic locations) being funded. He describes how these same companies fund the American Psychiatric Association and how psychiatric journals have become profitable because of advertisements taken out by the pharmaceutical companies. As I stated earlier, I don't know which bothers me more, the handful of unscrupulous executives and researchers or the large number of professionals who are blindly being convinced of a nonexistent validity by the large volume of poor research.

It saddens me that innocent parents have been roped into this game. CHADD (Children and Adults with Attention Deficit Disorder), a national parent organization, is funded mostly by money from Novartus (Breggin, 1998), the company that manufactures Ritalin. To indoctrinate these parents, speakers and literature are presented to them as factual and valid that are actually nothing more than the tons of findings of the junk (unethical) research. Parents are not equipped to decipher what they are being taught. To them it all sounds impressive and very scientific. What better supportive army of believers to have bolstering the acceptance of a disease and the need for amphetamine treatments than ordinary, honest parents. These people are seeking real help for their children, and instead they are trained to accept their children's drugged, robotlike compliance as substantive improvement.

A Brief History of ADD-ADHD Disease Theories

The first person to speculate that children who were inattentive and highly misbehaving were diseased was English pediatrician George Still in 1902. As a physician he was trained to see everything as medically caused, and his interpretation of these children's behaviors was consistent with his medical orientation. Unfortunately, even though no supportive evidence existed, the disease theory for ADD and ADHD had its beginnings.

Around 1923 a breakout of an encephalitis epidemic left numerous children with this inattentive and hyperactive behavior pattern. Dr. F. G. Ebaugh concluded that perhaps a virus or the encephalitic virus itself caused inflammation or damage to the brain of children that resulted in this behavior pattern. Without proof and only as a guess, this speculation further fueled the disease notion.

In 1937 Dr. Charles Bradley noticed that stimulant drugs seemed to subdue the behavior of highly active and inattentive children. As I said earlier, this became known as the paradoxical effect because he believed that only in these hyper children do we observe this subduing effect. This theory remained popular until fairly recently when researchers began to discover that stimulant drugs produce this same effect on everybody and anybody who can get high and feel euphoric.

Are the simultaneous calming and energizing effects of stimulant drugs proof that they are correcting a chemical imbalance and therefore there must be a disease? Baldessarini (1985) calls this reasoning *allopathic logic*; Valenstein (1998) calls it *ex juvantibus* reasoning, meaning that because a drug produces an effect, there must be a disease. For example, if I drink an alcoholic beverage and my anxiety is reduced, does that mean I have a disease called anxiety? Both Baldessarini and Valenstein would view this type of reasoning as false, misleading, and invalid as proof of any diseases.

In 1947, Straus and Lehtinen proposed the idea that the cause of these behaviors was some type of minimal brain damage (MBD), but it was so minimal that no one could find it. This notion has also mostly disappeared.

The *DSM-II* was published in 1968 by the American Psychiatric Association using the term *hyper-kinetic reaction of childhood*. Many psychologists considered the term misleading because it sounded like or connoted a meaning like a disease. During that time period psychologists were not in favor of such pejorative (negative and implying disease) terminology, and the term was dropped.

As Seligman (1994) stated during the development of the 1980 version of the *DSM-III*, there was a strong current of feeling to move away from both pejorative connotations and from disease concepts that had no support. Researcher Virginia Douglas viewed the behavior problems as resulting from a deficit in attention. The term *attention deficit disorder* was settled upon. However, I still feel the terms *ADD* and *ADHD* are pejorative and carry a strong connotation of underlying disease.

BARKLEY'S DISEASE CAMPAIGN

In the late 1970s and early 1980s Russell Barkley (1981) began a tireless campaign to convince the American public and professional community that ADD and ADHD are diseases. At first he had no support, no evidence for his claim of disease. But as Breggin (1998) points out, a very poor piece of research was published in 1991 by research physician Alan Zametkin, who claimed to have found the magic bullet using PET scans to identify areas in the frontal lobe of the brain that appeared to emit unusual metabolic readings in adults who were formerly believed to be ADD or ADHD. This article has been completely discredited in scientific circles. In addition, PET scans are not accurate (Sedvall, 1997). Nevertheless, this event catapulted a number of researchers into beginning the use of a cornucopia of new medical machines to produce volumes of widely diverse claims. No study merits credibility, but the sheer volume of studies seems to be winning over misguided and misinformed believers.

There Is No Diagnostic Test for ADHD

In 1998 the National Institutes of Health (NIH) held a consensus conference in an attempt to make sense of the overwhelming volume of material. The team of expert researchers made the following statement in their summation report: "At this time, we do not have a diagnostic test for ADHD (biochemical, physiological, anatomical, genetic, etc.). Therefore the validity of the disorder continues to be a problem" (p. 3).

Nevertheless, the ADD-ADHD "pharmacological industrial complex" continued to grow subsequent to this report. Russell Barkley is representative of the confusion, the contradictions, and the misleading statements and claims that represent the total lack of science that has created the quagmire in which we now find ourselves. Unfortunately, the children are the victims. Closely examine the following statements Barkley (1993, 1995) made:

ADD and ADHD are diseases . . . [1993, video].

Children whose problems with attention, overactivity, and lack of inhibition reach a certain level have a developmental disability known as *attention deficit/hyperactivity disorder,* or ADHD [1995, p. vii].

We now understand that many children with ADHD have an inherited or genetic form of the disorder, that many do not outgrow their problems by adolescence [1995, p. viii].

ADHD children look normal. There is no outward sign that something is physically wrong within their central nervous system or brain. Yet I believe it is an imperfection in the brain that causes constant motion and other behavior that people find so intolerable in a child who has ADHD [1995, p. 17].

I believe the disorder stems from under activity in an area of the brain [1995, p. 19].

ADHD may simply represent a human trait and not a pathological condition in most cases. As we just saw, which of us end up with ADHD seems to be determined much more by genetics than by environmental factors. In that sense, ADHD may be viewed as height, weight, intelligence, or reading ability, to name a few traits that are largely (but not wholly) genetically determined: . . . we differ in how much of it we inherit. . . . What is considered "abnormal" for any trait is simply a reflection of where we draw a line on the continuum for a trait, we label them as having a disorder. Such labels not only are based on a somewhat arbitrary measure but also obscure the fact that those with ADHD do fall along a dimension of normal abilities. To put it another way, we all have a degree of this ADHDtrait, and those with ADHD simply represent the extreme [1995, p. 65].

This means that ADHD should not be considered some grossly abnormal pathological condition—in fact it is a condition not qualitatively different from normal at all [1995, p. 65].

Finally, note this piece of rhetoric:

Misled by research reports that lab measures have found differences between ADHD and non-ADHD children and by the fact that ADHD is a biologically based disorder, many parents ask for medical tests to confirm the diagnosis of ADHD. At present there are no lab tests or measures that are of value in making a diagnosis of

ADHD, so blood work, urinalysis, chromosome studies, EEGs, averaged evoked responses, MRIs, and computed tomography (CT scans) should not be used routinely in the evaluation of ADHD children [1995, p. 122].

In this last statement, Barkley is saying that researchers can use these machines to make allegations of diseases or biologically based disorders, but these same machines can't be used in the clinic or office to confirm the presence of a disease. It is routinely OK to give kids risky drugs but not routine to diagnose the disease for which the drugs are freely given.

Do you get the feeling that you've been had and that the researchers pursuing this disease thing to justify the use of drugs are kind of scary? I have a unique perspective. I have a high rate of success in treating so-called ADD and ADHD children with properly designed behavioral methods—and no drugs. This makes it easy for me to state that there is no disease. I think that these are normal kids who are highly active and who hate school work! They are IA-HM (inattentive and highly misbehaving; see my proposal for a new, clearer diagnostic label at the end of the chapter). If better behavioral treatments had been developed earlier, we probably wouldn't be going through this absurd battle, with all this tongue-twisting psychobabble.

The Genetic Issue

Genetic and DNA research can appear very impressive. Even in this arena, however, it can be shown that the same tactics are being used to overwhelm the public and the professional community. The public is highly impressed with DNA research; it sounds magical and mystical. If the researchers can't convince the public or scientific communities with their disease theories, perhaps they can do so with the new strategy of using baffling DNA theories.

Again volume is superseding quality, and no study has gained acceptance or recognition (Joseph, 1999; Stein and Baldwin, 2000). Refer to the list that follows, and once again it is evident the plethora of studies that try to implicate a wide variety of DNA and genetic possibilities. "Junk science" (DeGrandpre, 1999; Joseph, 1999) or "unethical science" (Stein and Baldwin, 2000) is evident here as well. It is my hope that you, the reader, are beginning to question what you have been told and led to believe for the last twenty years.

Here are some of the gene and chromosome studies of ADD-ADHD.

Gene Implicated	Author and Date of Article
Fragile X	Samango-Sprouse, 1999
Dopamine transporter	Comings and others, 1991
Dopamine 4-D receptor	Comings and others, 1991
Dopamine B (hydroxylase)	Comings and others, 1991
Dopamine D2 receptor	Comings and others, 1991
Serotonin 1A receptor	Comings and others, 1991
Tryptophane 2, 3 (dioxygenase)	Comings and others, 1991
Monomine oxygenase, A & B	Comings and others, 1991
C 4B	Odell and others, 1997
DAT 1	Cook, Stein, and Leventhal, 1997
Monosomy AX	Samango-Sprouse, 1999

PROPOSAL FOR A NEW LABEL

Let's set all theorizing about causes aside and look at a practical matter: labeling children as ADD or ADHD is serious business. This label will suggest that they have a disease for the rest of their life. They will have to live with the mistaken belief that they can never be normal and that they will always have to live with a permanent defect that affects their entire lives and their ability to ever function normally. These children are stuck with a label that contains not one shred of truth.

Because words have such powerful connotative meanings, they influence the way we perceive and interpret events and concepts, so I suggest new terms for ADD or attention deficit disorder. Let's call it IA (inattentive). For ADHD or attention deficit hyperactive disorder, substitute the term HM (highly misbehaving).

Notice the change in your perceptions. To me the terms IA *and* HM help move our interpretations away from the pejorative disease label to a more realistic thought and behavioral disorder. Therefore, for the remainder of this book, IA and HM will appear alongside the traditional ADD-ADHD label. I hope the terminology will have an impact on both the public and professional communities and will begin to change our perceptions of these behaviors as diseases.

A QUIZ

What have you learned from this chapter? Answer the following questions to find out:

1. For what purpose was the Federal Drug Control Act designed?

_____

_____

_____

2. What types of drugs are categorized in Schedule I of the FDCA?

_____

_____

_____

3. Which drugs are categorized in Schedule II? Why?

_____

_____

_____

4. What are the risks of stimulant drugs?

_____

_____

_____

5. What is cognitive toxicity?

_____

_____

_____

6. What effects do stimulant drugs have on children's growth?

_____

_____

_____

7. What medical or psychological tests are used to diagnose ADD
   or ADHD?

_____

_____

_____

8. List the proof that ADD and ADHD are diseases.

_____

_____

_____

9. What does Russell Barkley say causes ADD and ADHD?

_____

_____

_____

10. After reading this chapter, what do you believe about IA-HM
    (ADD-ADHD)?

_____

_____

_____

_____

In the next chapter we'll explore the conditions that truly underlie children
behaving rudely and not paying attention in school.

3

THE REAL CAUSES OF IA-HM (ADD-ADHD)

Are you beginning to agree that IA and HM (ADD and ADHD) are not medical conditions and that there is no proof of any underlying disease? In this chapter we'll review the real reasons we have millions of children who do not pay attention in school and who refuse to respect the rules of proper conduct in both the classroom and in the home.

I believe that the behavior we are observing is not caused by a sudden epidemic of some mysterious disease that never existed before and exists nowhere else in the world but that modern social and familial problems are destroying children's beliefs, their ability to think, and their motivation to do well in school and to respect authority. And one of the ways I try to understand how these social and familial problems affect our children is to look at the problem from the perspective of cognitive psychology, as developed by Aaron Beck.

HOW COGNITIONS CAN BE CAUSES

Aaron Beck (1991), who is considered one of the most important psychiatrists in modern times, states that psychology is in a cognitive revolution. Cognitions are the thoughts, beliefs, values, and motivations that underlie behaviors. None of us engage in any acts that are contrary to our beliefs. If we scream angrily at someone we love, it may be because *we think* they have engaged in a behavior that is wrong and perhaps hurtful. If we race our car to a destination, it may be because *we think* we are going to be late for an appointment. Being continuously unhappy about our standard of living may be caused by an underlying belief that *we think* we should be rich and it is terrible if we aren't. So it seems clear that if children behave in an inattentive and disrespectful manner, it's the product of irrational and faulty thinking—what they think and what they value. In other words their behavior is caused by their cognitions.

In my work with IA-HM (ADD-ADHD) children I have consistently found five underlying cognitions. These children

1. Do not think.

2. Hate school work.

3. Neither focus on nor care about the future.

4. Hate reading. (I've had a few cases of children who loved reading, but they were the exception.)

5. Do not respect authority figures.

Let's take a look at each of these cognitions.

Not Thinking

IA-HM (ADD-ADHD) children bluster from one situation to the next without cognitively processing the impact of their behavior on others and without being concerned about the consequences of their behavior. They are neither actively vigilant nor observant of their surroundings. In part this is a motivational problem. They simply do not care what their behaviors do to or mean to others.

In Chapter Five you will begin learning the specific steps of the Caregivers' Skills Program (CSP), which is designed to require IA-HM (ADD-ADHD) children to learn to be thoughtful and vigilant. Controlling behaviors only is insufficient in ameliorating IA-HM (ADD-ADHD) patterns. Indeed, that is all pills do. The more essential part of a well-designed parenting program is to help children think actively. Our goal is to alter the unmoving inertia of their minds to a more active and very alive state of interaction. The CSP is designed for that very purpose.

Hating School Work

If you make the mistake of asking an IA-HM (ADD-ADHD) child if he likes school, he will give a misleading response: "Yes." But the correct question is this: Do you like school work? Many of these children actually enjoy going to school to be with friends or to participate in a number of fun activities. But when it comes to the academic work, they will clearly state that they hate it. All the scientists who search for mysterious diseases had to do was simply ask that question, as I routinely do. Almost universally and in no uncertain terms, the children will reply that they hate school work.

This is a motivational problem. The value and love of learning aren't important; these children lack the essential values needed to sustain them through each school day and through the long educational years. School work isn't easy. It takes strong values for children to want to focus on what to them is difficult and anxiety producing. Education means years of being tested and years of being hunched over a desk wrestling with difficult class and homework assignments. Education means mastering difficult concepts that frequently require considerable sweat, energy, and labor. Parents must instill a love of learning and education to curtail a child's inattention and misbehavior in school. Chapter Twelve shows how that can be done.

Not Focusing on the Future

These children don't think even two minutes ahead, much less ten years. They are not motivated by goals for the future. To them, going to college or becoming a professional is a meaningless abstraction. A few of these children may give consideration to these goals but give no consideration as to how they might achieve them. Their future is something that will just happen. They are focused on having fun—now. There is no connection in their minds between what's happening today and where they will be, either personally or professionally, in ten years. Remember the pop song, "All I Want to Do Is Just Have

Some Fun"? This could easily be the theme song for ADD-ADHD children. Self-discipline and hard work are not part of their cognitive repertoire, but having fun all the time is.

Hating to Read

Excellence in reading is perhaps the most essential skill for success in school. Very few ADD-ADHD children enjoy reading; most hate it. In Chapter Twelve, twelve specific steps will be covered to help your child develop a love for reading.

Disrespecting Authority

Too many children lack respect for authority figures. ADD-ADHD kids are often so labeled because they will not do what an adult tells them to do. Do you find yourself repeating commands over and over again until you are literally blue in the face? This is not because your child has some mysterious disease that prevents him or her from being mindful and respectful. It's because the child lacks the value that adults should be respected. Such children haven't learned the meaning of courteousness. They are experts at either tuning out or, in many instances, being oppositional and defiant. (And by the way, the so-called experts are now thinking about calling *defiance* a disease also. Will there ever be an end to this nonsense?) You will find the CSP to be very strict, but you will learn to get your child under control and to be respectful toward you, his or her teachers, and all other adults who deserve to be treated with respect.

I grew up in one of the toughest neighborhoods in New York City. Typically, we had the fight of the day. But when addressing an adult—any adult—we did so with courtesy and respect. Where did this mysterious disease come from—this disease that prevents children from showing proper deference toward adults? Which DNA strand suddenly mutated to cause so many millions of children to act disrespectfully toward adults?

If you train your child to think actively, to love learning, to love reading, and to respect authority, she will never become IA-HM (ADD-ADHD). If she is currently labeled as IA-HM (ADD-ADHD), you will learn in this book all that is necessary to instill new cognitive and behavioral patterns in your child and thus end the need for any such labeling.

A True Story: Mine

Until the age of twelve I was a wild and completely out-of-control kid. If the label had existed at that time, I would have been labeled as ADD-ADHD. Then two important events changed me. I became mesmerized by the TV show "Medic," starring Richard Boone. I wanted to become a doctor. And second, I began working in my father's small store in Hell's Kitchen in Manhattan.

Once I decided that I wanted to be a doctor, I started taking school very seriously. I became a straight-A student. It was important for me to hide my newfound academic seriousness from the other kids, however. I continued to act tough. The toughest kids were made class monitors in order to keep the other kids in line. I was a lieutenant of the monitors.

In order to work in my father's store, I began riding the subway. I didn't like the dirty surroundings, and I soon learned that the easiest way to shut out the environment was to read. Once I discovered the world of books, I became a voracious reader.

At my father's store I became friends with a homeless person named Teddy. I didn't learn until many years later that at one time he had been an esteemed professor of political science. He eventually explained to me that he gave up on life after he lost his family to Hitler's blitzkrieg on Czechoslovakia. He would come into the store to escape the cold. I'd often give him free coffee and a donut, which he consumed while we discussed my readings. He knew all about the books and authors I was reading. He made my readings come alive. I suspect that at one time he must have been a brilliant and exciting teacher.

His love of learning was, for me, contagious. I began riding the subway more and more to start taking advantage of all the marvelous cultural and learning institutions New York had to offer: natural history museums, art museums, libraries, theaters, rare book shops, and on and on. I think I must have read every plaque under every display in New York. Today my love for learning and reading define me as a person. I hope my passions are being passed on to my children.

Please note how my childhood change in attitude toward learning and reading, as well as developing a goal to be a doctor, totally changed my cognitive and behavioral patterns. I believe that such a change is possible for most children.

THE DISEASE OF MODERN SOCIETY

Perhaps it is not the children who have a mysterious disease. Perhaps we do. We, as adults, may be failing our children; we may actually be the carriers of the ADD-ADHD epidemic. Perhaps we are failing to teach, nurture, and instill a strong set of important values that are essential for children to be goal-oriented, love learning, respect adults, love the quiet of enjoyable reading, and be thoughtful and reflective. Are we the ones failing to instill the values necessary for succeeding in school? What is happening in modern society that is injuring our parenting abilities? Why are we not reaching our children? Why are we settling on drugs as a quick fix, as opposed to making the long commitment of nurturance, patience, and love that is so essential for the proper teaching of values? This is the crucial question each of us, as parents, must answer: Will we go for the quick and dangerous fix, or are we committed to long-term hard work, devotion, persistence, and loving care?

EXERCISE

Answer the following questions by checking the Yes or No boxes:

	Yes	No
1. Do you eat breakfast together as a family?	❏	❏
2. Is a parent at home when your child returns from school?	❏	❏
3. When your child was pre-school age, did one parent stay home to raise him?	❏	❏
4. On most weekdays, does your child have free-play time after school?	❏	❏
5. Do you eat dinner together as a family, with the television off?	❏	❏
6. Is one hour reserved each evening for quiet family reading time?	❏	❏
7. Does your child watch less than one hour of television each weekday?	❏	❏

	Yes	No
8. Do you sit to chat with your child for ten or fifteen minutes at bedtime?	❏	❏
9. Do you have quiet talks with your child several times each week?	❏	❏
10. Do you reserve the Sabbath day for unhurried family time?	❏	❏
11. Do you, as a family, regularly attend worship service?	❏	❏
12. Does the extended family—grandparents, aunts, uncles, and cousins—live reasonably close (less than two hours driving time)?	❏	❏
13. Are there frequent family get-togethers (about four or more per year)?	❏	❏
14. At least once a month do you, as a family, take fun, perhaps educational day trips together?	❏	❏
15. Do you have a clear set of values that you live by and that you teach your child?	❏	❏
16. Do you and your spouse enjoy a close, positive, and meaningful relationship?	❏	❏
17. Is your child enrolled in only one extracurricular activity per season?	❏	❏
18. Can you describe your own and your family's lifestyle as relatively serene and peaceful?	❏	❏
19. Is learning important to you?	❏	❏
20. Do you convey to your child that learning is an important value?	❏	❏

If you answered no to more than ten items, congratulations. You are an official member of the Diseased American Society Club. As a prize you have an excellent chance of having one or more children labeled as ADD or ADHD.

This is not meant to hurt you. It is meant to open your eyes so you can understand that we, as a society, are in danger of losing control of our lives.

Children need strong values, and the teaching of those values requires close, deep parent-child relationships. The questionnaire summarizes all the things we, as parents, should be answering yes to if we wish to teach our children a deep set of values. Children with deeply ingrained values such as loving to learn, loving to read, and respecting authority do not become IA-HM (ADD-ADHD).

WHAT HAS HAPPENED TO US

Children need an enormous commitment of time, energy, and nurturance to become emotionally healthy. Sadly, the state of our society is so structured that it is extremely difficult for parents to fulfill all their children's needs.

When I was a graduate student in the early 1970s, we were taught that a major part of our future clinical work would involve helping people cope with excess leisure time. Supposedly the onslaught of miraculous technologies was going to free up human labor and leave us with too much leisure time. Ha! It didn't quite work out that way, did it?

What has happened to American society has seriously affected what has been happening to our children. The events that have contributed to the 500 percent explosion in the numbers of IA-HM (ADD-ADHD) diagnoses since the 1970s are not mysterious diseases. They are the result of a societal-cultural breakdown that markedly impairs our ability to help our children adopt strong values in order to perform well in school and behave respectfully toward others.

See if the following makes more sense to you as causing IA-HM (ADD-ADHD) behaviors than an obscure disease no one can find. Place a check mark next to the circumstances that apply to you.

❑ 1. *The overwhelming daily schedule*
Are you a two-parent working family or a working single parent? Since the 1970s changing economic forces have made it a requirement for both parents in 85 percent of two-parent families to work full-time jobs merely to afford basic necessities such as a nice house and two cars to get to work in. And if you are a single parent, the situation is even more difficult and stressful, need-less to say. In such circumstances daily schedules can become harried and over-

whelming. Parents rush in the morning, leaving no time for breakfast and no time to calmly interact with their children. Many children are left to lock the house and go alone to catch the school bus. After school, they return to empty homes where they are unsupervised, possibly tuning in to trash TV shows. Parents may return home later, tired and edgy. They may communicate in a crisp way, giving orders and harsh commands for children to help complete dinner and straighten a messy house. Many families eat dinner while watching TV; often the children are in their own rooms watching their favorite shows. Rushed homework, baths, and bedtime stories leave little time for parents to interact with their children, so they can't grow close and instill deep values in them.

When children fail to learn these values, they don't care about quality school work and they don't develop respect for authority. The modern trend is to label them as ADD-ADHD (IA-HM) and control their lack of motivation and misconduct with the quick fix of pills.

❑ *2. Loss of the extended family*

The extended family used to consist of grandma, grandpa, aunts, uncles, and cousins who frequently came together at large family gatherings. This family constellation was once an important source for transmitting values, but, sad to say, this form of American life is rapidly becoming extinct. Most children no longer have an extended family to act as an important and powerful resource for learning values. We live today so far apart from each other, so isolated and often alienated from those who should be closest to us.

❑ *3. Moving*

Moving is the primary reason for the loss of the extended family. Twenty percent of the U.S. population moves from city to city each year. For children, moving away from family and close friends can not only be unsettling but can shatter their motivation to care about things. Why care, when they're going to lose it? Care and loss are too painful. Moving has made it almost impossible to hold the extended family together. Perhaps for one or two generations a few family members may fight to have family get-togethers once or twice each year, but disinterest inevitably wins out and the family closeness evaporates. If a child loses his extended family, friends, and familiar surroundings, consequent indifference and loss of caring can translate into disruptive behavior and loss of motivation to learn, culminating in being labeled ADD-ADHD (IA-HM). But there's hope. Solutions will be covered in this workbook.

❑ 4. Media

When children come home from school to an empty house, what TV shows do they tune into? Might it be Jerry Springer, Ricky Lake, or MTV? What values do these trash shows teach impressionable children? Do the messages in these shows include irreverence for authority, the unimportance of (or even hate for) school, familiarity with casual violence, and sex, sex, and more sex? Do impressionable children adopt these values? Yes indeed they do. Do these ugly values translate into indifference and misconduct in school? Again the answer is yes. Is this pattern of behavior more and more frequently being called ADD-ADHD (IA-HM)? Once again, yes. Is constraining their bad attitudes and misbehaviors with pills a meaningful and substantive solution to this problem? No. Do children learn anything from pills?

❑ 5. Divorce

Our young grow up in a world very different from the one we grew up in. Part of this change is in society; the divorce rate now is reported to range from 50 percent (Yax, 2000) to as high as 67 percent (Gallagher, 1989), and the number of children being raised by single parents is 50 percent (Yax, 2000). Today children are not only affected by their parents breaking up but by the terrible war that often ensues. Two sane people become jungle animals when they are divorcing; they are motivated to do anything to injure the other, often with considerable indifference to what this conflict does to the children.

Surviving the first few years of warfare does not end children's problems. Years of living in separate households often follow; the households may be run with disparate child-rearing philosophies. Such circumstances can be confusing to children. Learning a set of clear and cohesive values under these conditions rarely occurs. Children wind up confused about what is right or wrong. Values become muddled when the two people who are raising children act as if the other person is insane or a mortal enemy.

Why shouldn't a large number of children disrespect authority when ex-posed to such role models? Why should children care about a future when the now is a living hell? Why be well behaved when parents aren't? To make matters worse, the children are blamed for being uncontrollable, given a label that implies having a disease, and then given powerful chemicals to constrain them.

So why are so many professionals who should know better seeing "diseased" kids? Actually, it's the society around them that is diseased. Why are the professionals blaming the victims? What amazes me even more is that there aren't even more than the 10 percent of children now called ADD-ADHD when so many are being raised under the conditions I've described.

I'm a divorced dad, and I am not proud of it. Fortunately, my ex-wife and I work well together to raise the children. We coordinate daily what must be done to get the children's needs met. Both of us place the children as a priority, and both of us are very close to them. We do almost all that is suggested in this book to make certain that the children grow up with a strong and healthy set of values. I make certain that I'm at their dive meets, their swimming competitions, their school plays, and so forth. Every day we have quiet talks. Their values and their emotional health are priorities for their mom and for me. Are those your priorities as well? Or do you think pills are the answer?

❑ 6. *Peers*

Even if you are the most perfect parent in the world, the parents of your child's friends may not be. As children grow closer to reaching adolescence, they increasingly adopt the behavioral patterns and values of their peer group. If the peers care little about school and even less about respect for authority, then their values may become your child's values. I'm amazed at the number of parents I meet who know little about who their child's friends are. Later in the book we'll discuss how to help your child become involved in healthy friendships.

There is an important flip side to peer relationships that I want to highlight: ADD-ADHD (IA-HM) can be quite obnoxious. As a result these children often become targets for teasing and taunting. The more a child reacts emotionally, the more favored he becomes as a target. Thus the teasing exacerbates the

ADD-ADHD (IA-HM) behavioral patterns. The teases and taunts can be merciless, harsh, and very cruel. These kinds of interactions are emotionally scarring to the children on the receiving end and equally harmful to those on the delivery end; these bullies develop an unhealthy insensitivity toward others.

No child wins in this type of exchange. But most teachers and principals are not taking specific steps to curtail these practices. As far as I can see, character education in schools is only being given lip service. Nothing substantive is being done. Please note how frequently teasing and taunting was a precipitant to those children who picked up guns and shot others in the recent rash of school shootings in the United States. Research (McGee and De Barnado, 1999) has shown, in fact, that 100 percent of the eighteen school-based multivictim homicides from 1993 to 2001 were enacted to take revenge against perceived bullying, disrespect, and harassment.

This is a national problem that must be dealt with. I want parents who read this book to become proactive. Work in your community and at your child's school to require that character education and sensitivity training be part of the school's curriculum. Children must learn to treat other children with love and kindness. We can't wait for one more child to die. Please. I ask that all of you make this happen now.

Have you also noticed in the news that many of the children who killed were on psychiatric medications? Some blame the drugs for contributing to the occurrence. I don't think that is the real problem. I see the real problem in believing that pills would solve the problems these children had been facing. These killers needed more love and attention from their families. They didn't need pills to deal with being targets of relentless teasing and taunting. Schools could have been taking preventive measures by working with all the children. Teachers and counselors should have recognized the signs of children at risk. Perhaps counseling could have helped the parents to understand that they may not be giving sufficient attention to their child. Most important, counselors need to be proactive by not merely doing one-on-one counseling in their offices but actively conducting classes in caring for and understanding others. Children are not born with empathy; it is something they must learn. Parents, teachers, and counselors are the front line for instilling such important values.

WHAT WE MUST DO NOW

I hope you now believe that my thesis—societal and familial problems are plausible causes for the behaviors now identified as the dread diseases ADD-ADHD—is sound. There is a rapidly growing army of parents and professionals who are becoming disillusioned with the unproved disease theories and with use of dangerous drugs as the sole solution. I'm finding more and more support for my work. My office is being deluged with thousands of success stories using *Ritalin Is Not the Answer* as a resource. Now I hope this workbook will augment that book and help more and more parents work with their children.

Identifying the real causes of IA-HM (ADD-ADHD) behaviors helps pave the way for solutions. The Caregivers' Skills Program that follows will help you get your child under control. But that is not enough. It is only a start. Many changes must take place within your home and in your life to change your child permanently. Chapters Five through Thirteen will teach you the CSP, and Chapter Fourteen will help with solutions for improving time and communication while reducing stress, helping your IA-HM (ADD-ADHD) child love learning, helping your IA-HM (ADD-ADHD) child love reading, and helping your IA-HM (ADD-ADHD) child have better peer relationships.

When all this is finished, you will have a new child. You will hear yourself saying, "She's so much happier." I almost always hear this at a family's last session, which, by the way, occurs within two to four weeks after completing the learning of the program. But there's more. You too will be happier and more at peace. You will gain confidence in knowing that you're being the best parent you can be.

4

WHY THE
CSP WORKS

Have you been told that the best treatment for your child is a combination of behavioral methods with medication? Hundreds of research studies, plus a massive research project called the MTA Study (Multimodal Treatment Study for Attention-Deficit Hyperactivity Disorder), all make this claim: a combination of behavioral and medication treatments produces the best results.

But I can tell you this for certain: *current behavioral treatments do not work at all.* The only way they can work is if the drugs are added. In fact, using the drugs alone produces the same results. As I stated earlier, the drugs constrain behavior, calm anxiety, and improve focus and energize, all at the same time. The same thing would happen to you, dear reader, if you took a drug from the amphetamine family. This could be wonderful for everyone concerned, but the fact is that these drugs are the least healthy way to treat children. In addition, we are finding that it is difficult to stop the drugs because the misbehaviors immediately return. Children do not learn appropriate behaviors from pills.

Is there a better way—a real solution? Yes! That is what this book is all about. In Part Two of this book, you will learn the Caregivers' Skills Program (CSP), which produces real changes in your child—permanent changes. Your child will learn how to behave properly at home and at school, and his or her grades will improve dramatically without the need for any drugs. But before we discuss why the CSP works, let's consider why current conventional treatments don't.

WHAT IS WRONG WITH CURRENT BEHAVIORAL METHODS

If you have taken your child to a psychologist, I'll bet you've been told to follow most of the procedures I describe next. Place a check mark next to methods you've been instructed to use:

- ❏ 1. Post rules as reminders for proper behavior throughout the house.
- ❏ 2. Post the rules on color-coded cards.
- ❏ 3. Try to discuss with your child what he may be feeling when he misbehaves.
- ❏ 4. Count "one, two, three" before sending your child to time out.
- ❏ 5. Tell your child what she did wrong to have to go to time out.
- ❏ 6. Remind your child, while in time out, that he will not come out until he behaves properly.
- ❏ 7. Discuss with your child how she should behave before entering a store, restaurant, movie theater, and so on.
- ❏ 8. Sit with your child to help him with homework.
- ❏ 9. Ask questions designed to help your child organize her homework, such as what subject to do first, what needs to be read first, and so forth.
- ❏ 10. Try to prompt your child about correct answers to homework questions without fully answering the question yourself. (An example: "*Marco who* explored what country? His last name starts with a P. The name of the country starts with a C.")
- ❏ 11. Use a token economy program to reward your child for good behaviors; give check marks or stars on a chart that your child can accumulate for prizes or privileges.
- ❏ 12. When your child is misbehaving, ask how he should be behaving.

If you checked any of these, you are doing what is currently being recommended to most parents. Unfortunately, not only will these methods not work, your child will actually get worse. Then you'll probably be advised to place your child on drugs to improve school performance and conduct.

HOW CURRENT BEHAVIORAL METHODS MAKE YOUR CHILD WORSE

Currently popular behavioral approaches are based on a philosophy that ADD-ADHD (IA-HM) children are diseased and permanently handicapped and therefore require constant help. Parents are advised to post rules, constantly remind their child how to behave, help their child with homework, ask key questions to help their child organize, give warnings before disciplining, and so forth. As a sick, handicapped child, he needs constant assistance. This worsens your child by making him highly dependent in several ways:

- *He becomes task dependent.* The child cannot initiate, organize, or complete a task by thinking it through for himself. He becomes reliant on someone sitting with him, constantly cuing and coaxing. The child doesn't learn to think and problem solve on his own; instead he learns to mindlessly comply and copy. This actually increases the laziness of a child's thinking skills. He relinquishes the difficult problem solving to the adult and then merely robotically complies with what is instructed.

- *He becomes cognitively and behaviorally dependent.* This type of dependency occurs when the parent is instructed to ask his child to behave in a certain way before entering each new environment, such as a store, church, or restaurant. The child then fails to remember on his own; he will not learn to be attentive unless given assistance by being reminded. This also encourages mental laziness. And even after being reminded, he may still tear the new environment to pieces and forget everything that was mentioned before entering.

- *He becomes emotionally dependent.* Helping a child excessively leads her to believe that she must always have someone take care of her. It encourages her to believe she is incapable of being alone and have the confidence to function as an autonomous person. Becoming emotionally dependent is one of the worst handicaps we can perpetrate on a child. Later in life this can lead a young adult to make desperate choices for a life partner, to choose someone—anyone—to be there for her because she's too frightened to function on her own. ADD-ADHD children are already in a mess, and this type of dependency only perpetuates more of a mess in later life.

• *He becomes dependent on medication*. This does not necessarily mean being addicted to a drug. It means the child *believes* he cannot function without his drug. If a child takes a pill to function, he will develop the mistaken belief that he cannot function unless he takes his pill. Staying on the pill for many years makes it more and more frightening to stop; the child believes his entire ability to function will collapse. I see this all the time in college students who have been taking these drugs for years. They are terrified to stop. I've encouraged (with the help of their doctor) many students to try functioning without the pills. With a bit of encouragement and advice on note taking and study skills, most of my students have been able to get off the drugs completely without academic disaster ensuing.

• *She develops a life-long disease dependency*. Once told that she *has* ADD or ADHD, she probably believes that she will have this dreaded disease for the rest of her life. What a tragedy it is to have children believing that they are sick when nothing of the sort has ever been proven. The ramifications of this belief are unresearched, but one can imagine what may occur. Perhaps a child may not go to college, believing she doesn't have what it takes. She may settle on a poor marriage choice because, as a sick person, she doesn't deserve better. She may dream about but never become a writer because she can't think well enough for such a difficult undertaking. This list can go on endlessly. The point is that falsely believing one is mentally handicapped, when that is not true, is truly a crippling thing.

The good news is that the CSP is designed completely differently than currently popular approaches. It produces excellent results within a few weeks. The child learns to function independently. He gains self-confidence after discovering he can problem solve, he can control his behavior, he can remember how to behave, he can be a completely healthy and fully functioning autonomous person. He develops what Al Bandura (1986) calls a strong sense of self-efficacy, that is, the belief that he can overcome obstacles and take care of himself.

WHAT THE CSP IS

The CSP involves comprehensive parent training, designed to completely eliminate all IA-HM (ADD-ADHD) behaviors. It is based on the fact that there is nothing wrong with these children, that they can control their behaviors, they can actively think and problem solve, and they can perform well in school.

This is based on years of painstaking research and clinical development with hundreds of children. Since the publication of *Ritalin Is Not the Answer* it appears that my assertions have been validated. I've received thousands of letters from parents, teachers, psychologists, and physicians reporting their successes.

This mail has indicated to me that readers needed some clarification for some of the steps of the CSP. In fact, that is why I chose to write this companion workbook. I want to make it even easier for parents to learn all of the steps of the program properly.

This program is not a miracle. It works if you do. You must be willing to roll up your sleeves and carefully carry out all the steps. This workbook is designed to teach all the steps you need to know. The program is actually easy to follow. It is not complicated, and as you read through it, I think you'll agree that it makes sense. Once you see your child rapidly improving, you too will stop believing all this nonsense about your child having a disease and will stop relying on powerful drugs. You'll gain confidence in your skills as a parent, because you'll learn how to parent in ways that are healthy for your child. Your child will gain confidence, discovering that she is not diseased and that she can do all that is necessary to be well behaved and perform well in school. She'll discover that she can do anything she sets her mind to, with minimal help from others.

AN OVERVIEW OF THE CSP

Figure 4.1 shows the outline of the CSP. Each of the corners on the triangle represents the three main topics we'll be covering.

Target Behaviors

The bottom of the triangle shows the point at which we'll learn the specific misbehaviors, called target behaviors, that your child must learn to control. One of the major changes of the CSP is to focus first on your child fully controlling his misbehaviors *at home* before trying to improve his school behaviors. When we cover the specific behaviors, you'll probably react, as most parents do, by wondering if I have an X-ray machine that can see into your

Figure 4.1. The Caregivers' Skills Program.

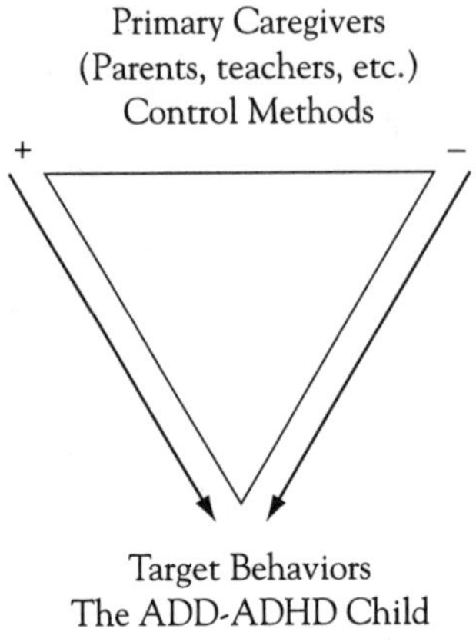

Primary Caregivers
(Parents, teachers, etc.)
Control Methods

+   −

Target Behaviors
The ADD-ADHD Child

home. I don't. But after twenty-five years of working with families, I've learned the specific misbehaviors in which IA-HM (ADD-ADHD) children engage. For most children, once these at-home behaviors are well controlled, school behaviors and attention problems improve automatically.

For the few remaining children you'll need to learn the Daily Report Card part of the CSP. This is Step Six of the program (Chapter Ten); it involves your child's teacher reporting your child's daily behaviors at school and academic performance, and *you* then carry out the consequences for any failures. Remember that the *DSM-IV* criteria for ADD-ADHD behaviors apply to behaviors occurring mostly at school. The Daily Report Card Program is designed to work on all those behaviors, in addition to those occurring at home. When this is done, almost all children improve a great deal both at home and at school.

Reinforcement

The upper corners of the triangle represent the consequences you will need to enforce to make these improvements happen. The "plus" (left-hand) side of the triangle represents how to reinforce your child to improve desired behaviors, pay attention properly, and develop an active, alert mind.

Discipline

Finally, the "minus" (right-hand) side represents the specific discipline techniques that are carefully designed to fully control all of the ADD-ADHD (IA-HM) target behaviors.

Within two weeks you will say, as almost all parents do, "He's well behaved, he's doing well in school, and he seems so much happier!"

Now you're ready to begin learning the CSP. I know you're anxious to get started helping your child—and yourself—become happier and more in control of your lives.

Part Two

THE CAREGIVERS' SKILLS PROGRAM

5

CSP STEP ONE: TARGETING BEHAVIORS

I'm calling this the first step of the CSP, although in a sense it is still prepara- tory. But targeting behaviors is such important preparation that it is integral to the program. Now is the time to figure out which of your child's behaviors you want to eliminate by using the CSP. We call those undesirable behaviors *target behaviors*. They are *observable, habitual, frequent,* and *inappropriate*. All children occasionally do most of the target behaviors we'll be reviewing, but it is unnecessary to work on a target behavior if it occurs rarely. If that is the case, do not include it in the list that applies to *your* child. However, if you are uncertain and cannot decide whether or not a behavior is occurring frequently enough, go ahead and include it. You'll soon learn that the CSP is a very rig- orous parenting program. If you must err, it is best to err on the side of thor- oughness.

THE CSP LIST OF TARGET BEHAVIORS

Seventeen target behaviors, which are divided into four groups, are included in the CSP program. You'll soon notice that the behaviors in Groups I and II are behaviors in which *your child manipulates you*. Yep, that is correct. IA-HM (ADD-ADHD) children manipulate their parents to get their way and to behave as they wish. The CSP program is designed to reestablish you as the boss. John Rosemond calls this being a benevolent dictator; the parent is a loving authority. In the CSP the children stop controlling events within the home. You do. You will reestablish yourself as the boss. Children need this structure to feel safe and secure. Underneath their defiant and sometimes cocky attitude, they really want their parents to be in charge. As this change takes place, you'll notice an obvious peace settling over your child.

Group III behaviors are the inattentive behaviors typically observed in ADD-ADHD (IA-HM) children. In the CSP this list is precisely and clearly defined and includes all the behaviors listed in the *DSM-IV* criteria under "control," at home as well as in school.

Group IV target behaviors are important but don't lend themselves to a conveniently labeled grouping; "other behaviors" will have to suffice.

A RATING SCALE FOR TARGET BEHAVIORS

Each target behavior will be explained, after the summary list, to help you decide whether a particular one applies to your child. In addition, I'll ask you to participate in a very important homework assignment. Space is provided next to each target behavior so you can rate how much each one has improved *during the previous week only*, compared to when you first started the CSP. Each week it is important that you return to this page and enter your new estimates *for that week only*.

I want you to make a subjective estimate of the percentage of improvement each week for each target behavior. Your rating will be somewhere between 0 and 100 percent. Here's what the ratings mean.

Ratings for Target Behaviors

0 percent:	No improvement at all.
25 percent:	Slight improvement.
50 percent:	Moderate improvement.
75 percent:	Good improvement.
90 percent:	Excellent improvement.

> *100 percent:*   You have seen no evidence of the target behavior during the previous week.

You may use any percentage you feel is accurate for each week, such as 66 percent or 43 percent. This is your subjective estimate.

If you are single, do these estimates by yourself. If you are married, do the estimates with your spouse and average your two scores. For example, if your estimate of improvement for a behavior is 34 percent and your spouse rates 66 percent, the average will be 50 percent, which is the number you write on the chart.

WHY THIS EXERCISE IS IMPORTANT

There are two important reasons for doing this exercise, so try to be as accurate as possible when making your estimates. First, school performance and conduct will not improve until you can honestly rate improvement on each target behavior above 90 percent. If you do not reach these high percentages, there will not be an automatic improvement in school performance and conduct. No school improvements occur, even if you must take the additional step of implementing the Daily Report Card Program (the last step in the CSP) without reaching this 90 percent level. Therefore, if you want school performance and conduct to improve, your goal is to get each at-home target behavior above the 90 percent improvement rating. (There is one exception: sibling fighting. I long ago gave up trying to get that one to improve as much as the others. But that's a subject for a different book.)

Second, when you have completed the first four weeks of the CSP, which should be enough time to get your child under complete control, I'd like you to send a copy of your rating page to me. This is purely voluntary, but if you do this, you will be contributing to scientific progress. Your identity will never be used, and you do not need to put your name or your child's name on the sheet. The data will be used for research, and all personal information will be held strictly confidential. Mail to Dr. David B. Stein, Department of Psychology, Longwood College, Farmville, VA 23909. To comply with ethical guidelines for research, approval for this project has been given by the Human Research Committee at Longwood College.

INSTRUCTIONS FOR COMPLETING THE TARGET BEHAVIOR RATING SCALE

Do your first ratings after completely understanding all the target behaviors and before starting the CSP. Ratings done before starting the CSP are called base rates.

Do the weekly ratings after you finish reading the entire book *and* after completing the first week of using the CSP. Then each successive week return to this table to enter your new estimates of improvement. By the fourth week your child should be well behaved at home and school, and his grades should all be passing.

But whereas your ratings will be finished by the fourth week, your work with your child will not be. It is essential that you continue being an active parent with the CSP until your child is twelve years old. By then your relationship should be so close and loving and his values so firmly entrenched that teen problems should be minimal.

UNDERSTANDING TARGET BEHAVIORS: AN INDIVIDUALIZED CHECKLIST FOR YOUR CHILD

Each target behavior will be explained. Be certain to reread each section until you fully understand the behavior. Use your imagination to paint a mental image of your child actually doing the misbehavior. Place a check mark in the box provided if the target behavior applies to your child. Remember that rare occurrences of the behavior need not be scored as a target behavior; we want to target habitual behaviors. If you are uncertain, go ahead and check the box as a behavior to work on. We want to be certain to help your child, so be thorough.

Group I: Active Manipulations

Try visualizing how your child uses these three manipulations to get her way. Clearly envisioning these behaviors will help you be more aware of their occurrence. Mention will be made after each description of how often these behaviors occur for IA (ADD) children and for HM (ADHD) children.

Table 5.1. Target Behavior Rating Scale.

WEEKLY RATED IMPROVEMENTS

Target Behaviors	Base Rates	Ratings			
		1st Week CSP	2nd Week CSP	3rd Week CSP	4th Week CSP

Group I: Active Manipulations

1. Not doing as told
2. Defying commands
3. Having temper tantrums

Group II: Verbal Manipulations

4. Making poor-me statements
5. Making negative-hostile statements
6. Nagging
7. Interrupting
8. Complaining about physical problems

Group III: Inattention Behaviors

9. Not paying attention
    a. Not looking
    b. Not listening
    c. Not remembering
10. Being helpless and dependent
11. Dawdling
12. Displaying poor reading skills
13. Performing poorly in school

Group IV: Other Misbehaviors

14. Tattling
15. Fighting with siblings
16. Being aggressive
17. Lying

❑   1. *Not doing as told*

IA (ADD): very common; HM (ADHD): very common

Do you find yourself repeatedly telling your child to do something, such as pick up his toys, until you scream in order to get him to comply? There is nothing wrong with your child that prevents him from doing as he is told the first time. He's tuning you out, either because he doesn't want to do what you are requesting or because he doesn't want to stop what he is doing at the moment. By arranging for the proper consequences, which you will be learning in the CSP, you can require that your child do as he is told without hesitation—the first time.

To help train your child to communicate assertively, allow him to ask politely if he may finish what he is doing. If your answer is no, however, require immediate compliance with your command.

When giving a command, do not yell. Speak in a moderate but firm and authoritative tone. One of the most frequent mistakes in modern parenting is to ask a child to do something as if you are apologizing. Remember: you are the parent-leader; speak as the authority.

Goal: One firmly spoken command, with the expectation of immediate compliance.

❑   2. *Defying commands*

IA (ADD): rare; HM (ADHD): very common

Does your child talk back to you? Does she glare at you defiantly? Does she say, "No, I won't"? Does she talk to you sarcastically? These are oppositional-defiant communications and should never be permitted.

Goal: Your child speaks to you respectfully and courteously at all times.

❑   3. *Having temper tantrums*

IA (ADD): rare; HM (ADHD): very common

Screaming, yelling, throwing things, and kicking furniture are unacceptable ways for a child to get her way. There is nothing wrong with your child that prevents her from disagreeing with you in an assertive manner. If you disagree with her point of view, the matter should be ended, without a tirade. If permitted, temper tantrums become worse with age, and for adults they can cause severe problems in life. Stop temper tantrums now!

Goal: No more than four or five temper tantrums, which seem to be associated with becoming ill or feeling extremely stressed, in a year.

Group II: Verbal Manipulations

These are the most overlooked behaviors for ADD-ADHD (IA-HM) children. These verbal patterns are often acted out in Academy Award–winning form by children determined to get their way. It often seems as if they are truly upset; these children are experts at these forms of manipulation. They use inappropriate verbal patterns not to express feelings but to manipulate you!

As you learn the CSP, you will soon understand that the practice of discussing children's feelings when they express one of these manipulative statements actually reinforces and increases their occurrence. If you allow this to continue, your child will begin to believe his own statements (this is called internalizing), and then he'll be unable to distinguish true feelings from manipulations.

Verbal manipulations can be subtle; you must remain alert for their occurrence.

❑   4. *Making poor-me statements*
     IA (ADD): very common; HM (ADHD): very common
     These are self-deprecating statements designed to make you feel sorry. Years of repeating them can underlie a child developing depression. If such statements are rare, treat them as genuine expression of feeling. However, if they are frequent, treat them as manipulations and permit no such statements for at least four months. After four months your child will be able to resume expressing them when they are expressions of true feelings, but be careful not to let your child revert to a manipulative pattern.
     Check the statements you hear often from your child; notice that whining, pouting, and crying are included and are to be targeted:

❑   You don't love me.
❑   You love my sister more than me.

❑   No one loves me.
❑   I can't do this. It's too hard.
❑   The teacher hates me.
❑   Everyone hates me.
❑   I'm ugly.
❑   I can't do anything right.
❑   The teacher never taught us that.
❑   I just can't understand math, and I try so hard.
❑   I'm stupid.
❑   School is too hard for me.
❑   You love the dog more than me.
❑   I want to die.
❑   I'm going to kill myself.
❑   (Whining)
❑   (Pouting)
❑   (Crying)
❑   *Add any statements that may be unique to your child.*

If you hear yourself describing your child as sensitive, the odds are she's skilled at making poor-me, manipulative statements.

I'll make a wager with you. I'll bet that statements like these are often made while your child is doing homework. I'll bet that he appears to be in agony, feigning an inability to do what the school has required. Sorry, but schoolwork requires deep concentration, memorization, and hard work, all of which your child may hate. Your child does not have a selective disease that allows him to play video games requiring deep intensity for hours but not permitting him to concentrate on school work, which he simply hates. He can play video games, and he can also do his school work. Soon you'll see.

Goal: After four months of permitting none, permit rare expressions of poor me if you judge the statements to be about genuine feelings. Two statements on the list ("I want to die" and "I'm going to kill myself") are almost always manipulations, but if you are uncertain, check with a mental health professional.

❑ 5. *Making negative-hostile statements*

IA (ADD): common; HM (ADHD): very common

Check those examples that apply to your child:

❑   I hate my brother.
❑   I hate school.
❑   Why do we always have to go there?
❑   Johnny's a creep!
❑   She's stupid.
❑   I hate you!
❑   You're mean!
❑   This is no fun.
❑   Life stinks.
❑   You never buy me anything.
❑   I hate boys. They should be on another planet.
❑   *Add other statements that may be unique to your child.*

Manipulative and unnecessary repetition of negative-hostile statements can underlie the gradual development of a very angry and cynical personality. These statements are considered manipulative because they may cause you to abandon something you've planned to do, or they may upset you, which may be what your child wants. Don't allow these to continue until it's too late.

Goal: Rare negative-hostile statements.

❑ 6. *Nagging*

IA (ADD): rare; HM (ADHD): very common

Why does your child continue repeating requests after you've said no? Because you eventually give in.

Goal: No nagging.

❑ 7. *Interrupting*

IA (ADD): rare; HM (ADHD): very common

As you learn the CSP, you'll begin understanding that children repeat behaviors that get reinforced. Annoying interruptions, whether in person or on an extension phone, are perpetuated as soon as you snap, "What is it?"

Monitor your reactions to interruptions; I think you'll see yourself reacting in exactly this way.

Goal: No interruptions, except in genuine emergencies.

❑   8. *Complaining about physical problems*
IA (ADD): fairly common; HM (ADHD): fairly common
Usually false complaints of not feeling well occur in the morning just before school and magically disappear right after school. Can you guess how these verbal manipulations get reinforced? I'll bet you can now anticipate what will happen to a child after years of engaging in this verbal habit? Does "hypochondriac" match your answer?

Group III: Inattention Behaviors

IA (ADD): very common; HM (ADHD): very common
Supposedly, inattention is the core of attentional disorders. Are you beginning to learn that inattention is only one part of a whole pattern of associated misbehaviors? Inattention is a habitual pattern, no different from any other target behaviors. This can be controlled as well as the other target behaviors, and when you finish your work with the CSP, you will no longer believe in mysterious diseases. Children don't pay attention because they hate doing chores, cleaning their room, and doing school work, and they don't behave properly because they don't respect authority and they neither think nor care about the impact of their disruptive misbehaviors on others. IA-HM (ADD-ADHD) are motivational problems, not diseases. There is no neurobiological problem with your child that makes it impossible for him to pay attention and be well behaved. You will know this when you properly carry out the work of the CSP and witness the changes in your child, without giving him drugs.

❑   9. Inattention is poorly defined in the *DSM-IV*. It must be defined in such a way that you can see it and hear it if you are to work on it. Therefore, it is necessary to dissect *inattention* into three discrete, observable components:

•   *Not looking (visual inattention)*: This is when a child does not keep his eyes on the task before him nor on the speaker talking to him.

Goal: Eyes should be on tasks when they are supposed to be.

- *Not listening (auditory inattention):* This is when a child is not listening; either she is tuning out the speaker, is daydreaming, or is listening to something other than what she should be. To confirm that your child is not listening, merely ask, "What did I just say?" An incorrect response will confirm your suspicions.

Goal: Correctly answering your question every time.

- *Not remembering:* The memory span of ADD-ADHD (IA-HM) children is a micro-nanosecond. They bluster from one activity to another without remembering what they should be doing. You'll soon learn that consequences to an incorrect response to the question, "Johnny, what are you supposed to be doing?" will soon restore memory skills.

Goal: Correctly answering your question and then behaving as he should.

❑ *10. Being helpless and dependent*
IA (ADD): very common; HM (ADHD): very common
IA-HM (ADD-ADHD) children are highly skilled at getting everyone else to do their work while they mindlessly comply with directions or copy what another person, usually an adult, has produced. They become highly dependent on individual attention and others helping them. Currently popular treatment approaches considerably exacerbate this problematic pattern. By treating children as diseased and handicapped and offering excessive assistance, helplessness and dependency are made worse.

Underlying helplessness and dependency are five major beliefs. Check the ones you may currently be instilling in your child:

❑ *Task dependency:* The child believes he cannot initiate, organize, or complete a task without someone helping him, and this mostly occurs with tasks the child hates, which, of course, includes school work. He will dramatically feign inability until he manipulates someone into helping him, which really means doing the hard work and diligent thinking for him. Current behavioral treatments recommend sitting with your child during homework, asking key questions to help him organize efficiently. The parent is also to sit with the child to prompt correct answers. Under these conditions the child mindlessly copies from the parent, exerting minimal mental effort and learning little, while the parent is the one who actually learns the material.

❑ *Cognitive-behavioral dependency*: In this form of dependency the child relies on others throughout any given day to remind her how to behave when changing from one environment to another. As recommended by current behavioral methods, before entering a store, or a movie theater, or anywhere, key questions are asked to help refresh a child's memory about how he is supposed to behave once inside. The child robotically reiterates the correct answers, only to forget within seconds upon entering the new location. Without real consequences the child will learn nothing and will do as he pleases. With the CSP, consequences, properly enforced, will ensure that a child remembers, as he should.

❑ *Emotional dependency*: When others do almost all of a child's work, she will increasingly believe that she cannot function on her own. Too much help diminishes belief in herself. She begins to believe that she *must* have someone in her life who will take care of her. Excessive emotional dependency creates conditions for desperately seeking partners, any partners, to be with her. This sets the stage for potential relationship disasters later in life.

❑ *Medication dependency*: This form of dependency doesn't mean drug addiction; it is a false belief that one cannot function without drugs—not a very healthy belief to live with, is it? And, of course, because currently popular treatments rely heavily on giving children drugs, this belief is becoming far too pervasive.

Claude Steiner says that making children dependent is the worst thing we can do to them. I agree. Excessive help diminishes a child's ability to develop the necessary skills to learn, which requires deep concentration and memorization. These are difficult skills that engender considerable anxiety and require great effort. To succeed, not only in school but throughout life, a child must master these skills, and to master them he must practice them. When we help too much, we deprive children of the practicing.

❑ *Disease dependency:* Has your child been told he has the disease of ADD or ADHD and that he always will? This is blatantly false and can be disabling for life.

Use the CSP to help make your child function well both at home and at school. Prove to him that he does not have, and never had, ADD or ADHD. When he can take pride in doing excellent schoolwork, he will know he is not ADD or ADHD.

Goal: To be as self-confident and as self-sufficient as possible.

❑ 11. *Dawdling*

IA (ADD): common; HM (ADHD): common

Is your child frequently late for school because he moves too slowly? Notice the selectivity of dawdling. When it is time to be ready for school, he'll be late. When it is time to be ready to play ball with his buddies, he'll be coaxing you to hurry up.

Goal: Be ready and on time for school every morning.

❑ 12. *Displaying poor reading skills*

IA (ADD): very common; HM (ADHD): very common

Most but not all ADD-ADHD (IA-HM) children hate reading as much as they hate school. Good reading skills are essential for good grades. In part their poor grades result as much from poor reading ability as from not paying attention. Steps you can take to motivate your child to love reading will be given in Chapter Eleven. It is very possible to turn this problem around. The most efficient way to improve reading skills is to read. The child who loves reading will read.

Goal: For your child to love reading and for you to frequently find him after bedtime under the covers with a flashlight, reading.

❑ 13. *Performing poorly in school*

IA (ADD): very common; HM (ADHD): very common

Problems in school usually underlie the reasons ADD-ADHD (IA-HM) children are referred to a psychologist and why most of them are put on drugs.

We have substituted fancy terms for ageless school problems. What used to be called poor conduct is now called attention deficit hyperactivity disorder, and what used to be called poor class performance is now called attention deficit disorder. When we used the old terms, we viewed the child as responsible for his behavior, but with the new terms, we blame it on some disease that doesn't exist. Using whatever terms are in vogue, we'll still get these problems under control with the CSP.

Goal: For your child to get the highest grades of which he is capable.

❑ 14. *Tattling*
IA (ADD): fairly rare; HM (ADHD): fairly common
Because they are obnoxious, ADD-ADHD (IA-HM) children are in frequent conflict with other children. Parental interference in their tiffs detracts from their solving their own problems and developing improved social skills. If your child tattles on someone as he asks you for help, it is best to respond, "Take care of it yourself." When, in the course of casual conversations with your child, the opportunity arises to suggest better ways of handling conflict, then by all means do so. But don't do this at the time of a conflict, because to do so adds to your child's dependence on you to fix things. The only permissible times for tattling are when someone is doing something dangerous, such as playing with matches, or a child is being aggressive.

❑ 15. *Fighting with siblings*
IA (ADD): fairly common; HM (ADHD): very common
Place any two people in close quarters for long time periods and, odds are, conflict will occur. Siblings constantly get on each other's nerves and can be expected to engage in ongoing battle forever.

There is a simple rule to follow: don't get into the middle of a conflict unless it becomes loud enough to disturb your peace and serenity. And if it does, never ask, "What's going on here?" If you do, you'll spend the rest of the day in *The People's Court*. Merely discipline both children, which you will soon learn how to do properly. If you hear them saying, "Keep it down or we'll get into trouble," you'll know you've reached the pinnacle of success with this problem behavior; expect to have it no more.

❏ 16. *Being aggressive*

IA (ADD): rare; HM (ADHD): occasionally

The only time aggression is permissible is in self-defense. Otherwise, even rare instances should not be permitted. If the regular CSP methods of discipline you'll soon be learning fail to control this sometimes tenacious behavior, you'll learn additional and more powerful ways to get this behavior completely under control. We certainly don't want anyone to get hurt.

ADD-ADHD (IA-HM) children may get into physical altercations because of teases and taunts. This does not justify a physical response. There is, however, something important you can do. Become proactive in your child's school to help put a stop to the teases and taunts, which have reached ruthless proportions among American youths. School programs in sensitivity training and empathetic caring must be started. School guidance counselors can do more than react to incidents one at a time. They can actively teach proper, caring values and behaviors. Parents and educators must join together in ending these horrible and hurtful practices. It is time that children stopped being scarred by awful mistreatment from others. Join me in this campaign, and let me hear from you about how your endeavors are succeeding.

Goal: No aggression, except in self-defense from physical harm.

❏ 17. *Lying*

IA (ADD): fairly common; HM (ADHD): fairly common

As with aggression, lying doesn't occur too often. But it must be brought under control as soon as possible because, with time, children can become increasingly skillful as liars. It is easiest to get this under control while your child is still young, so begin working on this while you can still easily detect that she is lying. I think you'll find that most lies involve school work: "The teacher didn't give us any homework" and "Teacher, I lost it on the bus" are common forms.

Goal: No lying.

Now that you fully understand all the target behaviors in which your child engages, go back to the Target Behavior Rating Scale and give your subjective estimates, before starting the CSP, about how problematic each behavior is for your child. Remember, 100 percent means it is not a problem, and a rating of 0 percent means the behavior is horribly out of control.

———————————

Now we will begin the work of learning how to use the CSP; you will learn the skills necessary for getting all these target behaviors fully under control *and* teaching your child to think actively, be vigilant, and be responsible for his or her actions.

6

CSP STEP TWO: IMPROVING DESIRED BEHAVIORS BY REINFORCEMENT

Sometimes my fellow psychologists criticize the CSP as being too strict and too repressive. Yes, it is strict, but it is not repressive. The CSP eliminates behaviors that prevent your child from doing her best and simultaneously improves the desirable behaviors that allow her to be the best she can be. If anything is repressive, it is the drugs that rob children of their spirit. The CSP is an enabling form of parenting.

In this chapter we'll take Step Two of the CSP. We'll learn how to enhance and enable desirable behaviors, that is, to reinforce good behaviors properly. *Properly* means that the CSP relies almost completely on natural, social, parent-child reinforcing techniques instead of on the payment of bribes, material reinforcers, and rewards. Stated simply, the CSP is a firm but *healthy* way to parent. I often hear parents say that the CSP makes so much sense that they use it effectively with their "normal" children. "That's the point," I reply to them. Your so-called ADD-ADHD child *is* normal. With proper parenting you will discover that he is no different from the other children except for hating school work, behaving obnoxiously, and being disrespectful of authority.

REINFORCE FIRST, DISCIPLINE LATER

Parents often want me to hasten into how to discipline, believing that discipline is key in getting these children under control. How to discipline correctly is important, but how to reinforce is even more important. Discipline only suppresses undesirable misbehaviors. It does not teach new and proper behaviors. Reinforcement is the key for making lasting changes in your child. Without actively reinforcing the behaviors we want your child to improve, we will be doomed to failure. No method of parenting will work unless you actively reinforce your child.

Twenty-five years ago when I first started working with ADD-ADHD (IA-HM) children, I taught discipline first, and my success rate was poor. I soon learned the importance of teaching parents to reinforce first; when necessary, I could teach them how to discipline later. My success rate immediately and dramatically improved.

TYPES OF REINFORCERS

The two broad categories for reinforcers are *social and material,* which can be subdivided into *activities and objects.* The following lists include examples of the elements composing each category; the importance of clearly understanding each category, especially social reinforcement, will become clear as we review their appropriate use.

Social	Material	
	Activities	Objects
Paying attention	Watching TV	Toys
Looking at	Video games	Favorite foods
Spending time with	Free play	Sweets
Talking to	Going outside	A new bike
Touching	Bike riding	Money
Praising	Special privileges	Tokens: check marks, stars, poker chips
Listening to	Attending ballgames	
Showing a reaction		

Preference for Social over Material

One of the most important features of the CSP is the almost exclusive emphasis on social reinforcement over material reinforcement. This is one of the most important departures from currently popular methods. The reasons for this are:

- Social reinforcement fosters close parent-child bonding; material reinforcement doesn't.

- Social reinforcement produces slower initial improvements but ultimately longer-lasting positive change; material reinforcement produces quicker initial improvements, which tend to fade rapidly.

- Social reinforcement does not foster a child developing *a payment expectancy* for proper behavior; material reinforcement does. Payment for proper behavior within the home should not become part of a child's expectations.

- Social reinforcement helps a child develop a positive self-image; material reinforcement does not.

- Social reinforcement provides a normal model for natural and healthy parent-child interactions; material programs are an inappropriate model for family and parent-child interactions.

Material reinforcement may be used in the CSP but only for particularly tenacious misbehaviors such as aggression or lying. If the need arises, activities are preferred before using objects as an attempt to avoid the payment expectancy trap.

Token Economy Programs

Currently popular programs emphasize a material reward system for IA-HM (ADD-ADHD) children. These programs are called token economies and involve giving children a symbolic reward such as stars, check marks, or poker chips, which are accumulated and later "cashed in" to pay for a variety of prizes such as favored activities, toys, or sweets. Obviously, these programs rely heavily on material rewards.

I view using token programs as a silly and unnatural way to raise children. The practice does not provide a healthy model from which children can learn family interactions. In addition, these programs teach the inappropriate value of paying children for behaviors within the home that should be natural and intrinsically rewarding.

Token economies also require that rules be posted and that some visible means, such as a chart, be provided to remind the child of how many tokens he has accumulated. The posting of rules and token charts provides excessive cuing for the children, thus requiring little effort on their part to remember how to behave and how to remain alert and vigilant of their own conduct. Such reminders enhance task and cognitive dependencies, something we prefer to reduce and eliminate completely.

When used in schools, a token economy program can be a useful tool for the classroom management of large numbers of children, but in the home it is counterproductive and inappropriate.

REINFORCEMENT PRINCIPLES

If you wish to change your child's behavioral habits, it is extremely important that you understand the principles of *how* to reinforce. Try to envision doing each recommended step. Check the box before each principle when you feel you fully understand it:

❑   1. *Immediacy:* It is important that you time reinforcing; praise your child immediately after he does a correct behavior. This helps your child learn the association between behavior and reinforcement. If you delay, you may confuse your child into associating the wrong behavior with reinforcement; timing is crucial.

Examples: "Johnny, please pick up your toys." He turns to comply. "Thank you son, for listening to Mommy and doing as you were told." Or Johnny sits down at the dinner table; without hesitation you say, "Johnny, thank you for coming to the table so promptly and sitting so quietly. I'm proud of you."

❑   2. *Consistency:* If your want rapid change, you must learn to be very consistent in praising good behaviors. Inconsistency will only confuse your child. This is especially important during the early stages of learning a new behavior. After several weeks you may relax a bit, but if you relax too much and too soon, you'll notice your child becoming confused. So stay alert. Consistency also means reinforcing in all locations; it means that both parents must actively reinforce.

Examples: In the supermarket where Johnny is often a terror, you say the following: "Johnny, thank you for entering the store like a big boy. You didn't play with the automatic doors. I'm proud of you. You remembered not to touch anything without Mommy's permission. You are being so quiet while we're waiting on line, and you remembered not to push the cart into anyone."

❑ 3. *Shaping or taking small steps:* To improve complex, difficult-to-learn behaviors, reinforce improvements for small steps. Use this to teach your child many self-help skills such as making the bed, cooking, and vacuuming or for sports such as swimming, batting, or throwing a ball or for school skills such as cursive writing or reading.

Example: Teach Johnny, at age five, to make his bed. Say, "Johnny, show me how you can make a bed." He does a sloppy job. "That was a very good try. Now let me help you do it even better. Each day Mommy will teach you a new part. Today we'll practice the corners, at the bottom." Demonstrate. Then after he tries, say, "That was terrific. You did the corners so neatly and carefully." Next day, say, "Today we'll learn how to pull the cover evenly after the corners are done." Demonstrate. Then after he tries, say, "Look what a big boy you are. You did the corners and neatly pulled the covers. That was terrific. You deserve a hug."

Continue this pattern for each additional new step. At first this will be hard work for you, but it will be easier in the long run. Your child can now be responsible for making his bed each day and be proud of his newfound skills and responsibilities.

Using Descriptive Statements

When using social praise, use carefully worded positive statements that describe what behavior your child is doing correctly. You, along with most parents, may not realize that you use descriptive statements much of the time, but in a negative way.

Example of a negative: "Johnny, how many times do I have to ask you to put your toys away? Do you see the toys in the middle of the floor? Did I not tell you to put them in that toy box right over there by the closet door?"

Example of a positive: "Johnny, thank you for listening to Mommy. As soon as I asked you, you immediately picked up your toys and put them in your toy box. I'm glad you did as Mommy said the very first time."

Additional Steps for Material Reinforcement

There will be times to use material reinforcements such as when lying and aggression have occurred. If improvement within the home doesn't generalize to the school setting, it may become particularly important to add material reinforcers when your child begins the Daily Report Card Program, which I describe in Chapter Ten.

The previous steps still apply to material reinforcement; it remains important to continue socially reinforcing correct behaviors. But the following steps for material reinforcement are also needed. Again, visualize the behavior and check the boxes when you fully understand each step.

❑   4. *Identify meaningful reinforcers:* To make material reinforcers effective, correct identification is essential. Each child will have reinforcers he or she favors that are different from those of other children. Observe your child, and write down those activities he loves doing or those objects he favors playing with or using. It is too easy to assume that things you like your child will also like. This just isn't so. For correct identification, observing and recording are essential.

Example: Many years ago I worked with a ten-year-old girl who was almost completely out of control—a very difficult case indeed. The CSP successfully controlled all at-home behaviors, but school didn't improve. It was necessary to implement the Daily Report Card Program. Before starting this step her father distinctly said, "Nothing is reinforcing to that little girl!" The following week her parents came with a list that included eating ice cream, watching TV, riding her bike, and dressing up for church. Yet for several weeks, school did not improve. I was suspicious and asked the parents how they had composed the list. The father admitted that those were things he liked, so he assumed she did, too. This time they were sent home to observe, and they reappeared with a new list, which included chewing gum all the time, playing a radio at bedtime, playing freely and without supervision outdoors, and wearing old jeans. School performance and conduct immediately began to improve.

❏ 5. *Make no substitutions:* This rule requires that if your child loses the use of a reinforcer for a set time period, say from 3:30 to 5:00 P.M., no substitutions are permitted. If she loses free play, she may not watch TV or play with her dolls or even do her homework. If she plays with anything, she completes her time in time out. This rule differs markedly from currently popular approaches. It is designed for IA-HM (ADD-ADHD) children who are particularly difficult to control; the CSP is more rigorous.

❏ 6. *Make daily renewal possible:* In the CSP, each day is a new day. If a child loses a reinforcer one day, he can re-earn it the next day by engaging in proper behavior. Our goal is for the child to learn proper behavior, not to prolong discipline. In the CSP, each day allows for a fresh start, a new chance to reengage in proper behavior.

The prolonged loss of reinforcers is reserved for the particularly tenacious behaviors of lying and aggression; the topic is covered in Chapter Nine.

❏ 7. *Make no special purchases:* In the CSP reinforcers are removed that already belong to the child. Buying extra-special reinforcers teaches a child that she will be paid for good behavior—a value we do not want to teach. This also sets the stage for the too-easy temptation of taking the new object away when a parent becomes angry, and this is another bad precedent.

Contingency

Contingency is a fancy but important term that means to apply proper consequences, both reinforcement and discipline, with extreme consistency. Think of it as an if–then sequence:

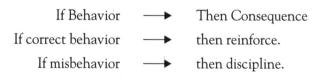

If Behavior	→	Then Consequence
If correct behavior	→	then reinforce.
If misbehavior	→	then discipline.

Examples: If Johnny sits quietly at the dinner table, then "Thank you for coming to the table quietly." If Johnny comes noisily to the table, then "Go to time out!"

You'll be reminded of this term in Chapter Seven when we review the principles for effective discipline. Remember: the principle applies for the immediate and consistent combined use of reinforcement and discipline.

In the next chapter we'll start learning an important lesson: *punishment does not eliminate misbehavior; discipline does.* I will make the difference between punishment and discipline clear. And I must remind you before we proceed that the reinforcement—the praise, the hugs, and the kisses—is the real key to success. Our goal is to win our children over, to motivate them. Reinforcement serves this motivational purpose. Without it, no methods of discipline will succeed; your child will not change. Work hard at being a reinforcing parent.

7

CSP STEP THREE: UNDERSTANDING THE DIFFERENCE BETWEEN PUNISHMENT AND DISCIPLINE

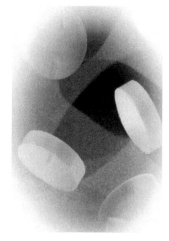

Few people are aware that punishment and discipline are not the same. Here's the basic difference:

- *Punishment* involves inflicting pain on children, usually in the form of yelling or hitting, as a consequence of their misbehaviors.

- *Discipline* involves using negative consequences, which are aversive but not painful.

In Step Three of the CSP, you will learn this difference through examples and then see how understanding what punishment is (and is not) can help you become a more effective disciplinarian.

EFFECTS OF PUNISHMENT AND DISCIPLINE

Consistent punishment does not reduce or eliminate misbehaviors—despite what desperate parents may think when they spank their child for misbehaving. Punishment often makes matters worse. Consistent discipline, however, when it is correctly designed, works extremely well and has few negative side effects. To see whether you are beginning to understand the difference between punishment and discipline—and to find out whether you might be punishing instead of disciplining—take a few minutes to give yourself the test that follows. The test and the results will be for your information and guidance alone.

SELF-TEST

Some of the following questions may be difficult for you to answer because critical self-examination is involved. I won't ask you to send me your answers. Only you need to know. Answer each question as honestly as you can.

Twenty Questions

	Yes	No
1. Do you spank your child one or more times per month?	❏	❏
2. Do you ever smack your child across the face?	❏	❏
3. Do you frequently threaten to spank or hit your child?	❏	❏
4. Do you yell at your child several times or more each week?	❏	❏
5. Does your child continue to engage in the misbehavior for which you frequently punish him?	❏	❏
6. Do you feel that yelling and hitting come easily to you, while praising and hugging feel odd and difficult?	❏	❏
7. Does your child seem nervous or anxious, displaying such behaviors as being jittery or fidgety, or stuttering?	❏	❏
8. Is your child a sullen loner who walks close to walls as if he doesn't want to be noticed?	❏	❏
9. Do you call your child bad names such as stupid, dummy, idiot, or retard?	❏	❏
10. Do you curse at your child?	❏	❏
11. Has your child had to see a therapist because of emotional problems?	❏	❏
12. Is your child an unprovoked aggressor toward other children?	❏	❏

	Yes	No
13. Is your child considered by others to be a bully?	❑	❑
14. Have you ever entertained the thought that you might be *physically* abusive toward your child?	❑	❑
15. Have you ever entertained the thought that you might be *verbally* or *mentally* abusive toward your child?	❑	❑
16. Have you had to yell louder and louder over the years to get your child to respond to you?	❑	❑
17. Have you had to hit or spank your child harder and harder over the years to get your child to behave properly?	❑	❑
18. Do you and your spouse argue frequently within earshot of your child?	❑	❑
19. Has your spouse ever hit you?	❑	❑
20. Has your spouse ever hit you while your child was present?	❑	❑

Score: If you answered yes to one or more of these questions, you may be a habitual punisher. You may also be contributing to your child's behaving like an ADD-ADHD (IA-HM) child. You definitely need to learn proper and more effective ways to discipline your child.

WHAT IS WRONG WITH PUNISHMENT

Not only does punishment not work to decrease or eliminate misbehaviors, in numerous ways it can actually make matters worse. I hope the following list of what typically goes wrong with the habitual use of punishment will convince you of the need to learn a better way. So important is understanding this list that I placed boxes before each item for you to check when you feel you have fully digested what can go wrong.

❑ 1. Punishment only temporarily suppresses a behavior. When the punishment stops, the behavior will return. Put another way, punishment is a suppressor, not a teacher. It does not teach children new behaviors. This is why punished misbehaviors keep returning.

❑ 2. Punishment's temporary suppression effect happens very quickly and therefore deludes the punisher into believing that what he is doing is effective. This rapid and immediate effect reinforces the punisher's behavior of punishing and thus contributes to establishing the act of punishing as habitual.

❑ 3. Consistent punishment can make a child anxious. The anxious child often displays agitated behaviors such as fidgetiness, excessive body movements and talking, difficulty sitting still, being easily distracted and edgy, and unable to focus and learn new things. If you connected that this sounds an awful lot like an ADD-ADHD child, it does. It *is* an ADD-ADHD child. Although most of these children aren't created this way, a significant number are. They can be created by excessive punishment, or already existing ADD-ADHD (IA-HM) behaviors can be considerably exacerbated. Making a child anxious in this way can contribute to many other emotional problems.

A True Story: Adam

I first saw Adam when he was eight years old. His teacher, who thought he was ADHD, initiated his referral. Indeed, he fit almost all the *DSM-IV* criteria: he couldn't seem to sit still; he frequently got out of his seat to wander around the classroom; he talked incessantly; he constantly bumped into others when in line; he called out incorrect answers; and he was performing poorly academically. After meeting his parents I became suspicious that Adam was a very anxious child. When I met Adam, my suspicions were confirmed. Adam's father was himself a very nervous and very stressed executive for an advertising firm. He constantly screamed at Adam, and sometimes, while in the car, he would become so enraged that he would pound the dashboard, honk the horn, and scream at Adam. Sometimes he slapped Adam across the face. Adam's mother was very passive, hardly ever challenging her husband's behavior. I chose not to start the CSP until *both* parents underwent therapy. Surprisingly, they consented readily. Therapy failed to take effect until the father had a massive heart attack and underwent quadruple by-pass surgery. Afterward he began to change. Finally, the CSP was implemented, and Adam made considerable gains—gains that would have been impossible if he had remained excessively anxious.

The anxious child does not learn well. Anxiety diverts a child's attention from his work to his personal problems. When he doesn't learn, the stage is set for even more punishment, creating a very ugly, negative cycle in which a child cannot win.

❑ 4. Other emotional problems can result from years of ongoing and excessive punishment. Withdrawal, depression, and anger are typical emotional consequences when living in a world filled with terror. Well-meaning parents may actually be unintentionally abusive. I'm often surprised when parents are surprised at being told this. If you answered yes to several of the items on the previous short test, I suggest some hard self-examination and soul-searching. Many of you, I'm certain, once you are aware of what you are doing will want to change. Perhaps the best expression of love for your child may be self-change. You can do it.

❑ 5. If you are punitive, you are modeling aggression as a way of handling your frustrations. What you model is often what your child will learn. Aggressive children often come from aggressive parents. Is this what you really want to teach your child? For most of you I know the answer is no, and you will be given healthier alternatives to work with your child.

❑ 6. If you yell, over the years you will have to yell louder. If you hit, over the years you will have to hit harder. As children adapt to pain, often at extreme levels, it takes more and more pain to get results. By becoming desensitized to and tuning out pain, punishment contributes to a loss of attentiveness; thereby exacerbating IA-HM (ADD-ADHD) behavioral and negative cognitive patterns even more.

❑ 7. Punishment reinforces the very behaviors a parent is trying to get rid of. Recall our list of the elements composing social reinforcement, and you'll soon notice that when you are yelling at and hitting a child, you are accomplishing most of these rewards.

Rewards	Present		
		Yes	No
Paying attention		❏	❏
Looking at		❏	❏
Spending time with		❏	❏
Talking to		❏	❏
Touching		❏	❏
Praising		❏	❏
Listening to		❏	❏
Showing a reaction		❏	❏

Look at the list carefully. Does it begin to make sense why your child endlessly repeats frequently punished misbehaviors?

A True Story: Bobby

Bobby was a three-year-old terror. His father was obviously embarrassed by Bobby's very annoying behaviors. He was everywhere at once while he and his dad were in my office. He touched things on my desk; he pulled books off the shelves; he even pushed a chair over. I told the father that by hitting Bobby he was actually reinforcing the misbehaviors. At our last meeting Dad told me he was ready to leave after that statement but that after successfully completing the CSP, he fully understood what I meant.

❏   8. There is another way to look at why children get punished and yet persist in the same misbehaviors. Stimulation can be conceptualized as being in three forms:

1. Positive stimulation (+): positive reinforcement

2. Zero stimulation (0): sensory deprivation

3. Negative stimulation: (−) punishment

Zero stimulation means an absence of stimulation on the senses and is also called sensory deprivation. Research shows that zero stimulation is the most aversive condition for adults and children. Children will do almost anything to avoid zero stimulation. If parents are not providing positive reinforcement and if children are avoiding zero stimulation, where will they turn for stimulation? You guessed it. They turn to negative stimulation, or punishment. Children will actually seek out punishment to be stimulated. I realize that this seems bizarre, but it is logical and is supported by research.

PRINCIPLES FOR DESIGNING EFFECTIVE DISCIPLINE

Now we can use what we know about punishment to help us design effective discipline. IA-HM (ADD-ADHD) children need discipline; they are very much out of control. It would be ideal if reinforcement alone were sufficient to control them, but such is not the case. That's why parents often resort to punishment in desperation. But as we've seen, punishment often makes matters worse.

Psychologists have developed three forms of discipline that are effective in some circumstances: (1) ignoring, (2) reinforcement removal, and (3) time out.

- *Ignoring* is the removal of social reinforcement.

- *Reinforcement removal* (RR; also known as response cost) is the removal of material reinforcement.

- *Time out* means removing the child from contact with all reinforcements.

Use of Ignoring and RR with IA-HM (ADD-ADHD) Children

Ignoring doesn't work with IA-HM (ADD-ADHD) children. Their behaviors are much too far out of control. Since the publication of *Ritalin Is Not the Answer* I've discovered, from my speaking engagements and discussions with parents, that I inadvertently confused them on the topic of ignoring. I included it in that book because I thought it would be useful as a way of demonstrating some general principles about discipline. I never intended for parents to use ignoring with IA-HM (ADD-ADHD) children. But parents indicated that they *were* using it and that it *wasn't* working. So I'll not discuss the topic here except to humbly make this correction and clarification: *Do not use ignoring with ADD-ADHD (IA-HM) children.*

RR—the loss of material reinforcers—will be discussed in Chapter Nine (it's Step Five of the CSP) for use in controlling the particularly difficult behaviors of lying and aggression.

Use of Time Out with IA-HM (ADD-ADHD) Children

If your reaction to the mention of time out was, "Is that it? Is that all there is?," you are again correct. If you tried time out and it didn't work, *it shouldn't have*. Time out, as presented by currently popular behavioral programs, theoretically shouldn't work. And it doesn't. As currently presented to parents by other authors, time out not only doesn't work, it makes matters worse. Here's why some currently popular approaches don't work. They recommend

- *Giving warnings before time out or counting "1–2–3" and then time out.* Warnings or counting make children reliant on the parent to remember when misbehavior is occurring. The methods you will learn in the CSP program require the child to remember.

- *Discussing a misbehavior before time out.* This inadvertently reinforces the misbehavior occurring at the time. You'll learn how to use time out to avoid any inadvertent reinforcing.

- *Ignoring behaviors until they reach more severe levels.* This reinforces testing behaviors, something you will learn not to permit with the CSP.

- *Rescinding the command to go to time out if the child complies with an excuse or a correct behavior.* This teaches children to push the limits on misbehaviors and to test how far they can go before getting into trouble. You'll learn to allow no testing.

Other mistakes will be presented in the full discussion of using time out for IA-HM (ADD-ADHD) children (see Chapter Eight). You'll learn to use a specially designed time out that allows IA-HM (ADD-ADHD) children to control their behaviors *and* trains them to actively use their minds. Everything you learn will be very different from what you may have been previously taught, so hang on.

Requirements for Effective Discipline

Immediacy, consistency, and *lack of humiliation* are three basic requirements if discipline is to work.

Contingency is important as well. Remember that the consequences you administer should match a child's behavior. *If a misbehavior, then discipline; if a proper behavior, then reinforcement.* If you keep this sentence in your mind at all times, you will not fail.

Check the boxes when you fully understand each requirement. You'll have to remember them when you work with your child, but within a couple of days everything will come naturally. (If the first three sound familiar, it's because they are identical to what you read about in our discussion of reinforcement.)

❑ 1. *Immediacy:* Discipline misbehaviors immediately when they occur. Timing is important because you want your child to learn to associate reinforcement with proper behavior and discipline with misbehavior.

Example: If your son doesn't hear you tell him to pick up his toys without delay, he'll be sent to time out. He'll soon learn to listen carefully when you speak.

Example: If your son doesn't listen to you telling him to clean his dishes right after breakfast and you're in a hurry to get him to the bus, using time out after school only disciplines his behavior when he walks in the door, not the morning's noncompliance.

❑ 2. *Consistency:* Apply discipline for every instance of misbehavior, even at a mere hint of a target behavior (misbehavior). Consistency also means to discipline in all locations, such as stores, malls, and even church. To be completely consistent, both parents should discipline any misbehavior when *it occurs in his or her presence.* Avoid saying, "Wait 'til your father gets home!"

Example: If you discipline your son for noncompliance at home but not at the store, he'll learn not to listen to you whenever you're in a store. You must be consistent in all locations.

❑ 3. *Lack of humiliation:* Discipline should be carried out so that you avoid embarrassing or humiliating a child. If you're in public, carry out discipline as discreetly as you can. Far worse, however, is the misuse of discipline to deliberately humiliate a child.

Example: Don't discipline your child openly at a family gathering. Do it quietly and discreetly to avoid embarrassment.

Example: Don't make your child face a wall for time out when in a public place. To do so is very humiliating and completely unnecessary.

A True Story: Mark

I first saw Mark when he was seven years old. He fit the classic profile for ADHD. At home he was noncompliant and defiant; he had severe temper tantrums at least two or three times each week; poor me's occurred several times each day; negative statements were constant; other misbehaviors included dawdling, nagging, and interrupting. In school he was constantly in trouble for talking with other children, not completing work, throwing spit balls at other children, and calling out; his grades were generally poor. The parents completed the CSP, but things did not go as expected. Improvements were not appearing. Since I couldn't figure out what the parents were doing incorrectly, I had Mark in for a detailed talk to try to pinpoint the problem. It became clear that Dad had a tendency to be abusive, which I didn't uncover in any of the previous sessions with Mark and his parents. Dad had painted a dot on the kitchen wall and required Mark to stand on his toes the entire time he was in time out. This was humiliating and abusive, which I strongly pointed out to the father. I told him that if he wished to destroy his child's soul, this was the way to do it. In addition, I told him that if it ever happened again, the authorities would be contacted. I don't think it was ever repeated.

❑ 4. *Lack of pain:* Discipline does not involve pain; punishment does. And we've already ruled out any consistent use of punishment when working with a child. The issue of spanking is controversial and will be discussed next.

Example: Screaming at the top of your voice is meant to be painful. This makes a child anxious and isn't necessary.

❑ 5. *Lack of anxiety:* Well-designed discipline doesn't make a child nervous. As we discussed earlier, making a child nervous defeats all the good things we are trying to accomplish. Constant yelling and hitting are guaranteed to make a child anxious.

❑ 6. *Active reinforcement of good behaviors:* Without active reinforcement no method of discipline or punishment will work. As with punishment, discipline suppresses behaviors; it does not teach new ones. It is reinforcement that teaches new behaviors.

Example: If your daughter immediately complies when you tell her to pick up her toys, say "Thank you for listening to me. You're so nice when you listen carefully."

❑ 7. *Zero stimulation:* As stated earlier, zero stimulation is most aversive to children. It can, therefore, be used for effective discipline, incorporating all the requirements we just reviewed: freedom from pain, humiliation, and nervousness. Zero stimulation equates to boredom, which entails the loss of contact with all reinforcers. Well-designed time out best approximates zero stimulation. But again, I must emphasize *well-designed*, which is what you will be learning in the next chapter.

THE ISSUE OF SPANKING

Spanking and yelling are punishment. They involve the application of pain as an attempt to decrease a behavior that a parent judges to be inappropriate. Are there times when spanking or yelling are justified? Formidable arguments can be made for each of the opposing sides on this very contentious issue. Murray Straus (1999) and Irwin Hyman (1999) present strong and very convincing arguments against ever using spanking. They offer noncorporal alternatives such as time out, loss of privileges, and effective parent-child discussions to resolve conflicting issues. I agree, in part, with their arguments; it is my preference that spanking never be used, if that is possible. I disagree that their methods are effective with very out-of-control IA-HM (ADD-ADHD) children.

Historically, neither spanking nor currently popular noncorporal methods of punishment have worked well with these children (Stein, 2000). In fact,

I've written (Stein, 1999, 2000) how currently popular methods of discipline for IA-HM (ADD-ADHD) children actually worsen their behaviors; some of the more important reasons were discussed earlier in this chapter. You will be learning noncorporal methods that are specifically designed for IA-HM (ADD-ADHD) children and are much more precise and rigorous than those proposed by these authors. And they will not worsen the behavioral problems.

Equally impressive arguments in favor of spanking are made by Robert Larzelere (1999) and DuBose Ravenel (1997). They favor a judicious and infrequent use of spanking when noncorporal methods fail to do the job.

As I stated, I prefer that whenever feasible spanking never be used. As you can clearly ascertain from my earlier arguments on punishment, the *consistent* use of spanking and yelling has major drawbacks. Spanking and yelling model aggression, reinforce undesired behaviors, cause anxiety, and increase a child's pain threshold, which enhances his ability to tune out. But in rare instances spanking—and even yelling—can be helpful. I have used spanking only one time with one of my three children. I would have preferred not to spank, but I believed the circumstance of Kevin, at age seven, running toward an accessible high-speed highway merited the spanking. My governing belief is that a *very* rare spanking or yelling can be used to make a lasting impression that the specific behavior went way beyond what is acceptable.

The four situations in which I think spanking or yelling has merit are these:

1. *When a child does a very dangerous behavior such as running between parked cars into traffic.* If a child makes a move toward traffic, and if it is observed in sufficient time to prevent a disaster, a noncorporal method of discipline should be sufficient. But if the child's movements present an imminent and clear danger, then a spanking can be useful for making a lasting impression. An example is when my son Kevin bolted toward a dangerous highway.

2. *When you are training a child to remain in time out.* You will probably never have to spank again. I have found that merely instructing a child that a spanking will occur if he fails to go to time out or if he gets out of time out is sufficient. Rarely has more spanking been necessary for any parents whom I have worked with. However, if you do not believe in spanking, a rigorous alternative will be given.

3. *When a child is being extraordinarily recalcitrant.* An example is consistently refusing to comply with Mom's requests when Dad is at work. A spanking by Dad or the knowledge that Dad will administer a spanking helps teach the child that matters will get worse if the child doesn't listen to Mom. I'm a realist, and during my nearly thirty years of practice I've encountered children who were extremely out of control and very recalcitrant. I have had cases where children would not, under any circumstances, obey Mom. But if the child knows that Dad will serve as an immediate backup, he usually will obey her. There have been instances of single moms whose ex-spouse was noncooperative and a surrogate, such as a granddad or an uncle, had to serve as a backup to help establish Mom as the authority.

4. *If a child is so wildly out-of control that even the rigorous CSP was failing.* In that case, after several weeks a spanking can help get the program started. In my entire career I've had, if my memory serves me well, four or five cases of such wildly out-of-control IA-HM (ADD-ADHD) children that even the very rigorous CSP could not get them under control, and a spanking was necessary to help get the program moving along. I might add that in each case it worked.

When and How to Spank

Here are some general rules for spanking:

1. *Spanking can begin at age two, but with great restraint, and should end at puberty.* Time out can begin for most children by age two. This is the period when children become highly mobile and inquisitive and get into everything. It is best to make the environment extremely safe to reduce parent-child confrontations, thus reducing the need for discipline. It is also best, at this age, to physically put the child in the time-out chair, something that should not be done after age three, and to physically put the child back if he gets out of the chair. Do not resort to spanking. However, physically putting him back can actually reinforce his getting out. If he repeatedly gets out of time out, a spanking may be necessary.

The purpose of spanking, should it be needed, is to train the child to go into time out and stay in, on verbal command. The idea is to never have to spank again. And in the event you have persistent behavioral problems or are just beginning CSP with an older child, the last-resort use of spanking is only advisable until your child is ten or eleven, the age of puberty.

2. *Spank one to three spanks, only on the bottom.* I suggest spanking two-year-olds only once on the bottom, using an open palm, and using three spanks for older children. More specifics will be given in our discussion of time out. *Never spank a child anywhere other than his bottom.* Hitting a child across the face is degrading and should never be done. The bottom is well padded and is the safest place to spank.

3. *Never spank when your anger is out of control, and never spank abusively.* It is extremely important that you be in touch with your own emotional state when you spank your child. If your anger is out of control, it is best that you not spank. If you do, you will probably spank too forcefully, perhaps even abusively. A spanking should be controlled enough to be somewhat painful but not severe enough to leave bruise marks.

I realize that spanking is very controversial. For years many children have been physically and emotionally abused in the name of discipline and punishment—a practice that fortunately has received a lot of exposure, opposition, and public remedy under the auspices of Child Protective Services and other family, societal, and legal interventions. Different cultures and traditions, however, have different attitudes toward the use of spanking, both pro and con. Most parents today don't do it, and corporeal punishment in school has been outlawed in about half of the United States. But I believe that if you feel that the rare use of spanking is appropriate and if you can apply it in a timely, focused, brief, nonbrutal, and nonangry manner, it can be applied without causing long-term damage.

Remember what I said earlier, though. It's the hugs and attention you give your child that will be key in getting his misbehaviors under control.

In Step Four of the CSP you'll learn another technique for changing your child's misbehaviors: time out. This is not the time out you may have heard about before. It's new and designed especially for IA-HM (ADD-ADHD) children.

8

CSP STEP FOUR: USING A NEW TIME OUT

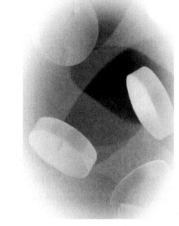

I mentioned earlier that we'd talk about a new and very effective time out. But you may be wondering: Why design time out differently for IA-HM (ADD-ADHD) children? There are two parts to the answer: (1) their misbehaviors are very much out of control and require particularly stringent methods to rein them in without resorting to the use of drugs, and (2) we need to activate their turned-off minds. Currently popular behavioral approaches do neither.

Recall our earlier discussions of the flaws built into currently popular approaches and about why these flaws contribute to the ineffectiveness of the programs. Drugs control the behaviors of IA-HM (ADD-ADHD) children but do not activate their minds. Their minds learn nothing from drugs; only their behaviors are suppressed. When attempts are made to stop the drugs, any gains disappear. This helps explain the trend for keeping children on the drugs for an increasing number of years, often well into their teen and early adult years.

If you've tried time out before, I respectfully ask you to clear your mind of everything you've been taught. Learn time out, as presented here, as if it were totally new, because it is. What you will learn is very rigorous and very necessary if you are to succeed.

A True Story: The Miracle Worker

In *Ritalin Is Not the Answer* I recounted a true story from the play, *The Miracle Worker*. It bears repeating here.

Teacher Annie Sullivan, hired to care for and teach the blind, deaf, and dumb child, Helen Keller, has difficulty doing her job because Helen's parents coddle her. With their misplaced sympathy and their belief that Helen is handicapped, they constantly interfere in the work Miss Sullivan must do. To make Helen function, Annie removes Helen to a small cottage behind the main house and away from her parents. Annie is a tough taskmaster; she believes that hidden under the cloak of silence lies an active and wonderful mind—and a real child. Annie gives no quarter, constantly requiring Helen to begin learning sign language. After a while the miracle begins to happen: Helen understands the sign for *water*. After that initial breakthrough, Helen begins learning at a remarkable pace, eventually developing into one of our great thinkers and writers.

Annie's tenacity and toughness were the kindest things she could have done for Helen.

Notice the mind-set Annie had: she believed in Helen. This is the same mind-set you must have with your child. You'll need the same sense of commitment, discipline, devotion, optimism, and faith in your child.

When I give speeches or workshops, I sometimes hear a parent say that she will try the program. I've been known to go on the attack when somebody says that. "No you will not!" I say. "You will *do* the program. You can't just try it; you must be willing to go all the way, or it will fail."

Are you willing to show the same love to your child Annie Sullivan showed for Helen?

THE STEPS FOR MAKING TIME OUT WORK FOR ADD-ADHD (IA-HM) CHILDREN

Carefully check the boxes as you review each step for using time out with the ADD-ADHD (IA-HM) child. It is essential that you make no changes or substitutions. What is presented here is deceptively simple, but every element is the product of years of clinical trials and research. No element is accidental; all are essential.

❑ 1. *Understand what "time out" means:* It means time away from access to all reinforcers. It is the application of total boredom.

❑ 2. *Designate a time-out chair:* Designate a comfortable chair as the time-out chair. Uncomfortable chairs should be avoided; that's unnecessary discomfort for a child.

❑ 3. *Locate the chair carefully:* The time-out chair is best located in a lightly trafficked room. A too-quiet room alerts your child when you check on him. A too-busy room is entertaining. If you have a formal living room, it would probably work well. If not, do the best you can.

❑ 4. *Avoid unintended reinforcers:* Make certain the chair is not next to a window; looking out can be entertaining. Make certain no objects that can be used as playthings are within reach of the chair; pens can be rocket ships and coasters can be flying saucers. Make certain the TV is neither visible nor audible from the chair.

❑ 5. *Do not use a bathroom for time out:* Several books recommend the bathroom as a good location. Not a good idea. Bathrooms have numerous things to play with, *and* they are filled with dangerous things such as pills and razors.

Clinical Experience: Never Use the Bathroom for Time Out

During my early career I learned the hard way that bathrooms were a very bad choice for time out. I had children who played *Star Trek* with the commode. On a couple of occasions parents reported flooded bathrooms, thanks to their child stuffing an entire roll of paper down the toilet. I've had children flood the bathtub just for fun; children seem to love finding out what will happen if an entire bottle of bubble bath is poured into the tub. It was common for children to try to find out how long a roll of toilet paper really is. And one child caused quite a panic when he flushed away all of his mother's birth control pills but *said* he swallowed them. This caused an unnecessary rush to the emergency room, not to mention Dad rushing to get Mom's prescription renewed. Is the point well made?

❑ 6. *Put the clocks away:* It is important that a child in time out lose all sense of time. He should not be wearing a wristwatch, and no clock should be visible from the chair. Have someone time you for ten minutes in the chair. To an active child this will seem like an eternity of unrelenting boredom, as it should.

❑ 7. *Use the minimum time in time out:* Do not experiment with varying times; the following minimum times work best:

Age	Minimum Times
two to four	3 minutes
four to five	5 minutes
five to eleven	10 minutes

These are minimum times. Under no circumstances should your child come out sooner.

❑ 8. *Be firm about time:* Your child should not be permitted to come out unless she is reasonably well behaved, with no crying, whining, begging, singing, yelling, pleading, or bargaining.

If your child is engaging in any misbehavior at the end of the minimum time, she must remain in time out. Wait until her behavior is reasonably close to perfect, then clock one minute extra before commanding her to come out. Coming out reinforces whatever behavior is going on at the time. If she is crying, you will reinforce crying. If she is quiet, you will reinforce quiet, which is what you want.

Example: Johnny is eight years old. He is sent to time out for noncompliance. At the ten-minute minimum he is begging to come out. You say nothing. Wait patiently. After nineteen minutes he finally becomes quiet; you clock one minute of silence and then command him to come out.

❑ 9. *Do not remind him to quiet down in order to come out:* If you do that, you will reinforce his misbehavior at that moment. If he is begging, your interaction reinforces begging; if he is crying, your interaction will reinforce crying. Remember Annie Sullivan, and stay firm.

❑   10. *Follow the bottom-of-the-chair rule:* This rule means that your child's bottom may not leave the time-out chair, and when he is told to go to time out, he must immediately go or his bottom is considered out of the chair. Some people find the enforcement of this rule to conflict with their beliefs about spanking. I discussed the two points of view about spanking at the end of Chapter Seven. To respect those who don't believe in spanking, I'll offer two alternatives, both of which work.

   a. *Use the spanking method:* If you are comfortable with spanking your child briefly and without anger or revenge, this method can work for you. As you read earlier, I am opposed to violent punishment because it doesn't work. But research has shown that the careful application of very controlled spanking can be effective in some circumstances. And remember that the purpose of spanking in this rule is to *never have to spank again.* This rule is to ensure that your child does not leave the chair and that he learns you mean business. Give three solid spanks on the bottom; wait until he stops crying, and reissue the command. If he still doesn't go, repeat the spanking. Spank no more than three times in a day, then let it go. Rarely does it go this far, once a child's been told what will happen. Usually the issue gets well settled after the first day.

   b. *Use a locked room:* The alternative method involves clearing your child's room (or any room) of anything that can be reinforcing. Place a lock plus a one-way peephole in the door to observe for safety. If your child does not immediately go to time out or if he gets out, he starts from scratch in the locked room. Apply all the appropriate time-out rules, as if he were in the chair.

❑   11. *Insist that the child go to time out immediately when told:* If your child does not go immediately, consider his bottom to be out of the chair and enforce the consequence.

❑   12. *Give no warnings: Never* give a warning. With this rule and the others that follow, you will begin understanding how strict the CSP is. Let me explain why. When a warning is given, it is the parent who has paid attention to the misbehavior. It is the parent who has realized the child is misbehaving. It is the parent who is being vigilant. It is the parent who is doing the active thinking. All the child does is mindlessly comply with the warning. The absence of warnings is one of the steps that helps activate the child's thinking and attending.

Currently popular is the "1–2–3 Time Out" method, which is a warning. This is exactly what you should *not* be doing. Indeed, your child will comply by the count of 3, but you will find yourself having to repeat the same commands day after day. This doesn't require the child to be vigilant, think actively, and remember the consequences should he let his guard down. In the CSP when no warnings are given, most misbehaviors disappear completely; the child will be remembering how to behave properly. To avoid the consequences your child will stay alert and vigilant. As you'll very quickly learn, he has nothing physically wrong with his brain that prevents his doing this remarkably well.

❑ 13. *Don't bargain:* Once the command to go to time out is given, you should not back down, even if your child says, "All right, Mommy. I'll pick up my toys." Send him to time out immediately. An essential part of the CSP is that you reestablish yourself as the boss. Other techniques recommend discussing what your child is doing wrong and what his feelings may be, which actually reinforces the misbehavior. Talking to your child at the time of misbehavior reinforces that misbehavior. Recall, if you will, that you are the parent-leader—the benevolent dictator.

Do not feel guilty about being in charge. With structure children feel safe and secure. They learn the boundaries of acceptable behavior, which is something ADD-ADHD (IA-HM) children have failed to learn.

❑ 14. *Practice rapid response:* To help associate discipline with misbehavior, send your child to time out at the time of a misbehavior. Do it immediately. Don't delay.

❑ 15. *Say, "Go to time out!" at the mere hint of misbehavior:* The rule for immediacy is even more stringent than you may have imagined. Target behaviors rarely go directly from good to bad. Escalation usually happens gradually, and often there are hints that misbehaviors are beginning to escalate. At the mere hint of misbehavior, such as a defiant look on your child's face when given a command to pick up his toys, the CSP requires that you immediately send him to time out. Remember that we are dealing with children who are out of control and who are not thinking. Being this tough gets their minds into an alert mode rapidly.

A True Story: Michael

Michael is presently an active case. He is nine years old and a very sweet child, with a wonderful smile. Michael is failing *everything in school* and is at risk for being held over. He fits the *DSM-IV* criteria for ADD. Although his parents are divorced, they are coming in together in response to this situation for his benefit.

Several weeks went by without any signs of improvement, and it was obvious that both parents were not following the CSP. Dad is very laid back, and Mom seems to be constantly busy with other things. The school authorities have been very insistent that Michael be put on drugs. I confronted both parents. I told them they had to make a choice: either start implementing the CSP or I'd refer them to other therapists who would most likely emphasize drugs. Both parents, not wanting Michael on drugs, agreed to get started. Soon it was obvious that they were letting many misbehaviors slip by and that they were not being alert for early signs of misbehaviors. Again we had a mild confrontation, and this time they seemed to understand the diligence the CSP required.

After two months they finally began to see results. The dad told me he realized that being a dad required more than just being his son's buddy. He realized that he was not fulfilling his role as a parent by letting things slip by. He now sees it as his duty to be Michael's boss. He now considers letting Michael fail at school to be shirking his responsibilities as a parent. Michael's grades are now passing, but it appears he will have to attend summer school, something he's not overjoyed with.

Divorce is difficult for everybody: Mom, Dad, and the child. The child gets bounced back and forth between two households, each with different parenting styles. Dads don't often get physical custody, and they often want to have special time with their child during brief visits. They frequently don't want the time spoiled with discipline. Mom may then look like the bad guy. It is best for all concerned if Mom and Dad can overcome their differences and unite as parents. It would help if *both* parents would read this book and coordinate parenting for the sake of their child.

❑ 16. *Do not talk to your child while he is in time out:* Once your child is in time out, it is imperative that you not say anything to him. Don't say, for example, "If you'd stop crying, I'd let you out sooner." If you do that, you will reinforce his crying, and he will repeat this on future days. This only confuses him.

❑ 17. *Never physically put your child in time out, and never physically take him out unless he is quite small:* Your child must learn to comply with your voice commands. Further physical contact abundantly reinforces his misbehavior. As little contact and interaction as possible helps to avoid reinforcing behaviors inadvertently. Do you understand the subtlety of reinforcement, that is, how even minor interactions can reinforce misbehaviors? Other behavioral approaches flagrantly violate many of these important subtleties. Inadvertently reinforcing misbehaviors is one main reason they not only don't work but actually make matters worse.

❑ 18. *Be sure to ask, "Why did you go to time out?":* Having a child think about what he did wrong is one of the important rules for time out. Don't repeat this to him every time he is sent. He is told this when instructions are initially given, and then it is his job to remember. We want to activate his mind. When he comes out, ask, "Why did you go to time out?" If he answers correctly, he must then perform the correct behavior. If, however, he doesn't answer and displays a marvelous award-winning act of being totally baffled, send him back to time out. You will now advance to the status of expert in child psychology, because you will learn that his act of bewilderment was just that—an act. After the second time out, he will give a full and accurate account of why he was sent there in the first place. This is how you learn that ADD-ADHD (IA-HM) children know considerably more than they let on and that they can feign the inability so expertly that they even fool the professionals. For those professionals who believe ADD and ADHD are diseases, I want you to carefully note children's skill at feigning ignorance.

❑ 19. *Require your child to perform the target behavior correctly after time out:* After telling you why he went to time out, he should then be required to perform the behavior correctly.

Example

MOM: Johnny, why did you go to time out?

JOHNNY: Because I didn't talk nicely to you.

MOM: Good, that's correct. How should you talk to me?

JOHNNY: Nicely.

MOM: Now, tell me what you wanted to say.

JOHNNY: Can I go over to Jimmy's house to play?

MOM: I'm glad you asked nicely, but dinner will be ready in half an hour. But since you did ask so nicely, would you like to go to Jimmy's after dinner?

There is nothing wrong with ADD-ADHD (IA-HM) children that prevents them from speaking to authority figures with courtesy and respect.

❑ 20. *Be absolutely consistent:* If you want results, it is important that you enforce the rules with absolute consistency. The CSP promises results, not magic; if you aren't consistent, don't expect your child to change. To fulfill the near-perfect consistency needed for changing ADD-ADHD (IA-HM) behavioral and cognitive patterns, be certain that consistency is enforced under these circumstances:

For every hint of a misbehavior

For every target behavior being worked on

In all locations and settings

Among all caregivers who spend significant time with your child, most especially your spouse or ex-spouse

Tip: How to Discipline away from Home

If you are at a gathering at someone else's house and your child misbehaves, send her to time out as discreetly as possible. Call her over to you and whisper in her ear, "I want you to go into the bedroom where the coats are and sit in the big chair, by the closet door, for time out." Carry out procedures as you would at home, but be discreet in order not to embarrass your child. She must learn that consequences will be imposed wherever she is.

❑ 21. *Enforce the universal law:* When giving instructions to your child about what time out means, be certain to include the universal law, which means that if your child misbehaves in a location where time out cannot be enforced, he goes to time out for a very long time when you get somewhere it can. The following are the recommended times:

Age	Time
three to four	30 minutes
four to five	1 hour
five to eleven	2 hours

Children can recognize when they have you cornered, and they may use these occasions to misbehave. Knowing that they face an extended time out usually eliminates these challenges.

❑   22. *Deal with dawdling:* The procedure just covered also applies to early-morning dawdling. You know that the school bus will arrive shortly, but there isn't much you can do about his deliberate slowness and his not being ready on time. But if your child knows he'd better be ready by a set time each morning or spend two hours in time out after school instead of playing with his friends, that usually ends dawdling as a morning problem.

❑   23. *Be comprehensive:* An important feature of the CSP is that you must use it to work on *all* target behaviors. Use time out for any suggestion of any of the target behaviors that apply to your child. If your child engages in a target behavior that isn't typical, use time out. When enforcing the CSP, *if you are going to err, err on the side of toughness.* Be thorough; be comprehensive.

❑   24. *Misbehaving on the way to time out:* What if your child immediately complies with going to time out but curses on the way or kicks a chair? When he comes out of time out, ask him why he went; then ask him what he did wrong on the way to time out? Then say, "Go back to time out!"

Example

MOM: Johnny, go to time out!
JOHNNY: Shit (talking under his breath while complying with the request).
MOM: (after the first time out is completed) Johnny, come out of time out. Why did you go?

JOHNNY: Because I wouldn't put my bike away like you asked.
MOM: Correct. But what did you say on the way to the chair?
JOHNNY: Shit.
MOM: Go back to time out! (and later) Come out now. What are you supposed to do with your bike? Go do it.

❑ 25. *Deal with sibling fights:* There are two considerations when handling sibling fights. First, never ask, "What's going on here?" Send all children involved to separate time-out chairs in separate rooms, with no questions asked. If you directly observed who the real instigator was, then only discipline that child.

Second, discipline sibling fights only when the decibel level reaches a point where your serenity is disturbed. If you discipline for every argument, your children will be in time out for life. Sorry, but that's the best I can offer for this one. If you have a better solution, write me.

❑ 26. *Don't fall for every bathroom request:* Any child who can hold it for eight hours at night can hold it for ten minutes in time out. But if you're convinced a plea is genuine, especially in a younger child, permit him to go and then start time out when he is finished. If an accident occurs, have him clean it up.

❑ 27. *Reinforce correct behaviors:* No discipline method will work if you fail to actively and consistently reinforce correct behaviors.

❑ 28. *Anticipate a behavioral burst:* When beginning to use time out as described here, you can expect that matters will get worse—lots worse. Your child will try everything she knows to get conditions back the way they were so she can have her way. Expect the behavioral burst (technically called an extinction burst). If it doesn't immediately occur, it will in a week or several weeks later. Be prepared.

The behavioral burst will last for several days. Then suddenly, by the fourth or fifth day, there will be a dramatic improvement in all target behaviors. When this turnaround happens, most parents are astounded.

❑ 29. *Don't settle:* By the end of the first week of the CSP parents are so happy at the dramatic results that they report their child is now wonderful. But that isn't enough. School problems will not improve until you go all the way. Recall our Behavioral Rating Scale, which I described in Chapter

Five. Only when all target behaviors have improved above the 90 percent mark will school conduct and performance improve.

☐ 30. *Explain time out twice:* Explain time out to your child only two times: (1) the night before starting and (2) at the end of the first day of enforcing it. It isn't necessary to repeat after that; children learn from experience. Keep the explanation simple and general. Do not review all target behaviors, because he'll remind you that you didn't tell him that.

Tip: Explaining Time Out

The explanation really comes in four parts. Here's part one: Johnny, from now on we're going to discipline you in a new way called time out. When you misbehave in any way, you will sit in the time-out chair for ten minutes. You must think about what you did wrong whenever you are sent to time out. If you can't tell us what you did, then you'll have to go back to time out to think about it some more. When you can tell us, you then must behave correctly.

Part two: If you misbehave in the time-out chair, you'll have to stay in the chair until you can behave like a gentleman. We won't remind you to behave; you'll stay in past the ten minutes until you remember.

Part three (option with spanking): If you don't immediately go to time out when we tell you, you will receive a spanking. If you ever get out of the chair without our telling you to, you will also get a spanking.

(Option without spanking): If you don't go immediately to the time-out chair, you will be sent to your locked room, where all your playthings have been removed.

Part four: Now you tell us what you've just been told. (Note: Keep the explanation general, nonspecific, and simple. Don't make it complicated or try to explain every detail.)

Allow him to explain and correct any misconceptions he may have. Repeat the end of the first day of enforcement, and never repeat again.

Ignore his reaction. Some children cry, some laugh, some act as if they don't care. They will.

FREQUENT MISTAKES

Now that you have learned about using time out, you are ready to begin using it in the CSP. Of all the behavioral problems that the CSP can address, lying and aggression are sometimes most difficult to control. In most cases they will be controlled by the CSP as you have thus far learned it. If after four weeks either behavior is still a problem, however, you'll need to add RR to the CSP— a special technique I've already mentioned; it will be presented in the next chapter.

I suggest you review everything we've covered to be certain you have a clear picture of what you must do. Be prepared for the behavioral burst, when everything will get worse. In fact, if you are doing everything correctly, you should get one whopping behavioral burst.

Real results should materialize by the end of the first week and definitely by the end of the second week. If by then you aren't seeing substantial improvement, *you are doing something wrong*. In my follow-up sessions, I'm present to critique what the parents are doing, and I'm skilled at finding mistakes. I wish I could do this for all of you, but that's unrealistic. Therefore, if you're married, you and your spouse critique each other. Be willing to take some criticism, but I hope you both do this exercise in a kind and constructive way. If you are not married, have a close friend read this book and then observe you. A third party often spots things you may not be aware of. Some of the most frequent mistakes include

- *Letting early testing behaviors slip past you.* You need to be more alert.

- *Not reinforcing almost every correctly done target behavior.* Be much more reinforcing.

- *Giving warnings.* Require your child to do the remembering. It is his brain we are training. Stop giving warnings or counting "1–2–3."

- *Being inconsistent.* This confuses your child and is unfair to her. Work very hard at being consistent.

- *Mom and Dad being inconsistent with each other.* You moms and dads should talk to each other and discuss when one is doing something incorrectly or is not working at the program. When that happens, your child pays the price. Do either of you want him on the drugs?

- *Not using time out for all target behaviors.* You must get your child completely under control. Failure to do so only hurts her. Keep that in mind at all times.

- *Being soft-hearted.* If you are soft-hearted, you are being cruel, because you are condemning your child to failure in school or being put on risky chemicals, or both. Constantly remind yourself of the consequences *to your child* if you are soft-hearted. Post the story of *The Miracle Worker* on your refrigerator as a reminder of what you must do. If you love your child, and I know you do, you will properly enforce the CSP to get her functioning at her best.

If all of your efforts using the CSP have so far failed to get lying and aggression fully under control, don't give up. In the next chapter we'll discuss special techniques for controlling these particularly tenacious behaviors: removing reinforcement. This is one way you can create negative consequences for your child without hitting or yelling.

9

CSP STEP FIVE: ELIMINATING LYING AND AGGRESSION BY REMOVING REINFORCEMENT

In most cases the CSP, as you have learned it so far, brings target behaviors—even intransigent ones like lying and aggression—under control. For the few cases where it hasn't, reinforcement removal (RR) is added to the CSP. It is essential to use the CSP before using the methods described in this chapter.

If after four weeks of enforcing the CSP all target behaviors are well under control except lying or aggression, go to Step Four of the program: use the RR method as *an additional technique* used exclusively to control these tenacious behaviors.

USING RR CORRECTLY

❑ 1. *Understanding RR:* RR involves the systematic loss, for long periods of time, of favored material reinforcers. Because lying and aggression are low-frequency behaviors, which means they usually don't occur often enough for immediate retraining, they may not necessarily respond to time out in the CSP. Adding RR has proved to be very helpful. Do not replace the entire CSP with RR; it is used as an addition.

❑ 2. *Using RR for lying and aggression:* Aggression—the use of physical force against someone else—doesn't occur frequently, usually less than once a month. Unless aggression is being used for self-defense, however, it must be stopped completely. Lying is difficult to stop because as children get older they become increasingly skilled at it, so it becomes harder to detect. It is best to stop a child's lying while he is very young. If a child does both behaviors, then both behaviors can be worked on simultaneously.

❏ 3. *Listing reinforcers in order of importance:* Make a list of at least seven reinforcers that are important to your child. To be certain what they are, observe him and write the reinforcers down. Both activities and objects may be used. Rearrange the list in order of importance, with number 1 being the most important, and number 7, although still important, the lowest on the list.

❏ 4. *Removing a reinforcer for each incident:* Then for each incident, take a reinforcer away, starting at the bottom and moving up the list to the more important items.

❏ 5. *Deciding how long:* The amount of time for the loss of reinforcers varies with age.

Age	Length of Time Lost
three to four	1 week
four to five	1 month
six to eleven	1 year

Some parents may see this as stringent, and indeed it is. But these are particularly hard behaviors to control, and neither should continue.

Case History: Andre

Seven-year-old Andre was considered by some to be the terror of the territory. He was a handsome little boy with a wonderful smile. But he was a hellion. When I saw him for his first appointment, he squirmed and wiggled in the chair for the entire appointment. One could easily conclude that it was impossible for him to sit still. At home he was very much out of control, manifesting almost every target behavior: noncompliance, oppositionalism, poor me's, with lots of whining and crying, negative statements, temper tantrums, and so forth. His teachers frequently called home, informing his parents about poor conduct and very poor grades; Andre rarely finished assignments. He constantly disrupted his classes by talking, interrupting, calling out, and doing just about every behavior listed for ADHD in the *DSM-IV*. Other children teased and taunted him relentlessly, and at times he reacted aggressively by hitting, biting, and scratching, as if he were completely out of control. After an evaluation by the school psychologist, school officials were adamant that he be placed on medication. His parents were desperate for help. After reading *Ritalin Is Not the Answer,* they began working with him. Because they had a history of inconsistency, it was very difficult for them to implement the CSP. It took much longer than usual to get results—more than eleven weeks. After getting Andre completely under control, except for his periodic episodes of aggression, it was necessary to enforce the Daily Report Card Program (the last step of the CSP; see Step Six). School grades, attention, and conduct improved greatly, but other children continued to torment him, and he continued to react violently.

His *parents* made a list of seven reinforcers; in order of importance, they included (1) skate boarding, (2) riding a dirt bike, (3) using the PlayStation, (4) watching TV, (5) playing with toy soldiers, (6) roller blading, (7) eating sweets.

The first aggressive episode occurred within the first week. He lost *all* sweets for one year. It was seven weeks until the next violent outburst took place as a reaction to teasing and taunting. In my office he and I talked about how very deeply the taunting hurt him; he often cried. I taught him some social skills to counter their abuse, but another incident took place within two weeks. His roller blades were taken away for a year, and he was not permitted to borrow skates. His reactions continued, resulting in the loss of his toy soldiers, loss of TV-watching time, and use of his PlayStation, each for one year. Dramatically, all violent incidents stopped. By the end of the school year, because he had changed so much, most of the other children began to accept him and stopped taunting him.

A few continued to deride him, but other children were beginning to defend him, telling the bullies to leave him alone. "He's really trying to be nice, so back off."

Andre passed all subjects. His temper tantrums and occasional violent episodes completely stopped. His parents stated at the last session: "He's a new kid. He seems so much at peace. Other kids now come to play with him at the house, and their parents are giving the new Andre a second chance."

———————————

If after four weeks of working with your child *all at-home behaviors on the Behavior Rating Scale honestly exceed 90 percent,* and if school hasn't improved, you are now ready to learn the Daily Report Card Program—the subject of the next chapter.

IO

CSP STEP SIX: USING THE DAILY REPORT CARD PROGRAM

You probably don't need to take this last step. Twenty-five years of clinical records, five years of research on the CSP, and thousands of letters from readers of *Ritalin Is Not the Answer* consistently indicate that if you have followed the program in this book diligently and exactly as directed, 80 percent of you have children who are now doing well in school, and no formal school intervention is necessary. For the other 20 percent, we have a bit more work to do. But take heart. The steps discussed in this chapter will help your child improve all aspects for doing well in school: improving conduct, improving class participation, passing all tests, and correctly completing all homework assignments.

Before continuing with Step Six, however, I must address a very important issue—brought to my attention by readers, in particular by physicians prescribing the CSP.

BUT MY CHILD IS WELL BEHAVED AT HOME

Immediately after *Ritalin Is Not the Answer* appeared on store shelves, physicians began contacting me to help unravel some confusion. It came to my attention that parents were reporting satisfaction with their children's improved behaviors at home, but school did not automatically improve, and the Daily Report Card Program wasn't working. Especially perplexing were parents who claimed that their child was well behaved at home but not at school. They didn't see the necessity for using the CSP.

As Winnie the Pooh might have said, "I thunk, and I thunk, and I thunk," but it took quite some time until the answer became clear. Here was the problem. For most of my years in practice I automatically administered the Behavior Rating Scale exercise (see Table 5.1 in Chapter Five) to parents. We would not proceed with any school intervention until all behaviors were subjectively rated as improved more than 90 percent. So automatic was this practice that I didn't think to write it into the book. It just didn't occur to me. That is why I made it the first step of the CSP (see Chapter Five) and have been repeatedly emphasizing in this book that *you must do the ratings exercise*.

However, there is an additional problem. Some parents may think their child is well behaved at home and doesn't need the CSP; these parents think school is the only place where the problems are manifested. In my administration of the rating scale, a clear pattern has emerged over the years. Some parents are somewhat liberal about what they consider good behaviors at home. However, their ratings indicate that their children's target behaviors usually cluster at the 50 to 70 percent level. Even if parents find this acceptable, the realty is that at these levels, school performance and conduct *will not improve*.

So I must then negotiate with parents about making a choice. If they steadfastly stick to their belief that these are sufficient levels for home conduct, they will face school authorities who hound them to put their child on drugs. And believe me, authorities in some school districts can be relentless. In a few locales, much to my chagrin, parents have been ordered by the court to comply with medically directed treatment and mandated to put their children on drugs! My solution is this: it is either my way or the drug way. I wish I had an alternate solution, but I don't. As long as this drug frenzy persists, and as long as school authorities are frantic to make kids behave perfectly and perform well, no other choices are available. These parents must elevate their home behavior expectations if they wish to avoid the drugs.

CHECKLIST TO USE BEFORE STARTING SCHOOL INTERVENTION

Hidden problems may underlie your child's inattentiveness or misconduct in school. Although teachers are usually good at detecting these problems, they can overlook them occasionally, so it is a good idea to have each of the following checked:

❑ 1. *Eyes and ears:* Have your child's vision and hearing tested.

❑ 2. *Level of intellectual functioning:* A school psychologist can test your child's intellectual level of functioning. If your school district does not have a school psychologist, the test can be done at a local mental health center or with a psychologist in private practice; other resources may be available in the community. Some children are slower learners than others. The possibility has to be considered that a child may not be able to keep pace in school with her peers, and this may also underlie inattentiveness and misconduct. She may be a slow learner and therefore unable to comprehend her current level of work. Although this is difficult for parents to face, once detected, their child can be placed in slower-paced or ungraded classes where she won't be tormented by not being able to keep up with the other children. Under proper classroom conditions she can learn well and lead a very productive life. (Note: Restrict the psychologist to administering the intelligence test, or you may end up with a child diagnosed as ADD or ADHD and then be pressured to place him on drugs.)

❑ 3. *Undetected learning disabilities:* Learning disabilities (LDs) mean that a child's overall intellectual functioning is at or above average, but he has difficulty understanding or learning in one or two subjects like math, spelling, or reading. LDs and ADD-ADHD (IA-HM) often occur together. An undetected LD can underlie a child's not paying attention and frequently getting into mischief instead of doing her work. However, the converse is more frequent: inattentiveness causes the learning problem. If a child does not pay attention in the earlier grades when fundamentals in specific learning areas are being taught, he may not learn the basics.

In many subjects if the basics are not well learned, progress in that subject will henceforth be perpetually impaired. A child with an LD will lag behind in one or two subjects while doing well in all others. Some believe that LDs are caused by brain abnormalities, but evidence for this theory is sketchy. The cause is not particularly important because remediation methods are uniform; they entail using a multisensory form of retutoring the basics in that subject.

Multisensory tutoring involves employing several of the senses during the learning process. For example, if a child misreads the word THINK as THNIK, the word may be written on paper with glue, sprinkled with sand, and allowed to dry. The child then relearns the word by tracing his finger over the sand (touch), saying the word aloud (audition), while looking at the word (sight). The child is then employing three senses in the relearning process instead of sight alone. There are sophisticated tutorial programs that teachers use, but this gives you the general concept. Once remediated, many children completely catch up in the subject with which they were having difficulty.

❑   4. *Sudden onset of IA-HM (ADD-ADHD)*: If IA-HM (ADD-ADHD) patterns suddenly emerge without having been present before, then a new problem may have developed in a child's life such as a school bully, his parents' divorce, or his friends suddenly turning on him. Resolution of the underlying conflict is usually sufficient to end the episode, and neither the CSP nor the Daily Report Card Program will be necessary.

THE DAILY REPORT CARD PROGRAM

School report cards are usually given every six weeks, which is too infrequent for reshaping new behaviors. To help your child, it is best that precise feedback be given daily to parents. The Daily Report Card (DRC), shown in Figure 10.1, is designed to give parents all the information they need, yet it is very easy for teachers to fill out.

Once again reader feedback has helped me correct another problem. Parents, physicians, and therapists have indicated that in a few instances, teachers refuse to cooperate, complaining that they don't have enough time to fill out the DRC. A step that has been helpful is to copy the following letter and give it to the teacher.

Figure 10.1. The Daily Report Card.

NAME: _____

DATE: _____

Subjects	CLASS PERFORMANCE (Doing work, Participation and attention)				CONDUCT IN CLASS				TESTS AND QUIZ GRADES (Returned Today)	HOMEWORK GRADES (Returned Today)	TEACHER'S INITIALS
	E	S	N	U	E	S	N	U			
1.											
2.											
3.											
4.											
5.											
6.											
7.											
8.											
9.											
10.											
11.											
12.											

COMMENTS: _____

_____

_____

_____

E = Excellent
S = Satisfactory
N = Needs Improvement
U = Unsatisfactory

Note: Permission is given by the author and publisher to make copies of the DRC for use with readers' children.

Dear Mrs. Jones,

My son Johnny has caused considerable problems in your class. In addition, he has not been paying attention, resulting in poor grades. As you are aware, he has been diagnosed as ADD-ADHD. In trying to avoid medication, I decided to use the Caregivers' Skills Program as presented in Dr. Stein's books, *Ritalin Is Not the Answer* and the companion workbook, *Ritalin Is Not the Answer Action Guide*. At home Johnny has dramatically improved. For most children the improvements at home automatically improve school performance and conduct. But in a few instances this does not happen. It is then necessary to coordinate with a child's teacher.

Unfortunately, Johnny is one of the few children who improved at home but not at school. To improve his school problems, I need your help. As outlined in Dr. Stein's books, all I request is that each day you communicate to me, through an easy-to-fill-out Daily Report Card, how my son has behaved in school. When I meet with you, I can show how the Daily Report Card only takes a minute or two to complete. I can then enforce the same consequences that improved his behavior at home to help improve his behavior in your class.

I know how hard you work and know that this request is an imposition, but as Johnny improves I believe the classroom environment will also greatly improve for both you and the other children. We should see improvements within two weeks to a month. Once he is doing well, the Daily Report Card can be stopped.

If this fails to work, we may then have to consider other steps. But having seen real results at home, I believe that if you and I work together we can help Johnny do well in school and avoid taking strong medications.

I thank you for your kind consideration and for your dedication as a very fine teacher.

Sincerely,

Keeping a Record of Grades

Some children become confused about grades. When asked how they are doing in school, they typically recall only the last two or three tests or the last two or three homework grades. If the last few grades are good, they'll report that they are doing well, forgetting all the grades that preceded these last few. Figure 10.2 is provided to display *all* grades. It is the child who must record her daily home and test grades, which are returned each day for each subject. Subjects are recorded at the top, and test and homework grades are recorded within the subject columns. This serves as a constant reminder of precisely how your child is performing in each subject. Meet with your child and teacher once each week to make certain the recorded grades are accurate.

Understanding the DRC

Once the teacher is willing to cooperate, all that is necessary each day is to give the teacher a new copy of the DRC. To help you and the teacher understand the design of the report card, check each of the following when you are clear what each part means:

- ❏ 1. *Column 1: Subjects:* In the first column list *all* subjects for *all* class periods. Be certain to include lunch, music, health, and physical education or anything else scheduled for the day. It is important to know how your child behaves all the time under all conditions.
- ❏ 2. *Column 2: Class performance:* When I was in graduate school, one of my professors taught me a very important lesson: "The rule for rules is to always keep them simple." He believed that the fewer words used in composing rules and the more simply they are stated, the more people will understand and comply with them. In composing the DRC I incorporated his advice. Instead of listing all the behaviors that encompass ADD, such as failing to keep eyes on work, daydreaming, not attending to questions, and so forth, I chose to place on the DRC an expression teachers have known and used for many years: Class Performance. It's simple, it's brief, it's to the point, and teachers know its meaning well. Choosing this simple descriptor appears to have been good because most of the children I've worked with have improved their class performance extremely well and, in turn, their so-called ADD symptoms disappear.

Figure 10.2. Record of Test Grades to Be Posted at Home.

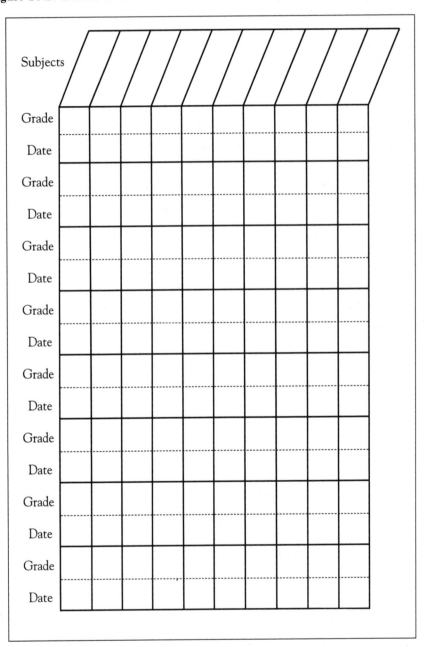

Note: Permission is given by the author and the publisher to copy and use the chart for personal use only.

❏ *3. Column 3: Class conduct:* To simplify the "H" (or hyperactivity) part of ADHD, I chose another old-fashioned and familiar term: Class Conduct. Teachers have always understood that children who call out, get out of their seat, push other children, step in front of others when in line, and so forth have been behaving badly in class and were labeled as having poor class conduct. Two words, used for hundreds of years, seem perfectly satisfactory to say what is intended.

Tip: The Importance of Changing Labels

Notice what has happened in the last twenty years. We have taken easy, honest, accurate, and direct terminology of performance and conduct and "medicalized" and "mystified" it into terms that connote diseases: attention deficit disorder and attention deficit hyperactive disorder. Because they connote diseases, these terms imply that children are diseased and handicapped and consequently not responsible for their behaviors. This has resulted in justifying the use of powerful drugs and has led to the development of ineffective behavioral techniques designed to treat the sick and handicapped.

However, using the terms *poor class performance* and *poor class conduct* on report cards implies that the child has been responsible for his behaviors and thus, as in the old days, deserved the consequences.

My hope is that the diagnostic terms will change to IA-HM (inattentive-highly misbehaving) and that the report card terms continue as they are to help eliminate the medical and mystical connotations of disease.

When you complete using your new tools to work with your child, rethink this issue.

❏ *4. Column 4: Test and quiz grades:* The fourth column is reserved for the teacher to jot down grades for any quizzes or tests that are returned each day. In this way you, the parent, don't have to wait anxiously for six weeks to know precisely how your child is doing academically. And you can match the consequences at home to daily failures in school. This should take only a few seconds for the teacher to complete. It is essential that the teacher be accurate. Readers have complained that a few teachers carelessly entered grades that did not match the real six-week report card. When this happens, it causes the wrong consequences to be given to the child, and progress will be halted. Teachers, please fill out the DRC accurately.

❑   5. *Column 5: Homework grades:* The teacher's accurate reporting of homework grades each day is as important as test grades. Again, consequences can then match the behaviors.

With the daily matching of homework grades and consequences, the homework hassle can stop. No longer will it be necessary to lock horns each evening to get your child to complete homework and do it well. The imposition of consequences will rapidly improve your child's homework skills—something you may have been told is impossible. Waiting six weeks to find out that your child is not doing homework properly is insufficient for shaping proper skills.

With the DRC program, as well as with the CSP, it is essential that you not sit with your child while he does homework. You can remain nearby and serve as a resource to answer questions or to help direct your child to where answers may be found. It is also essential that homework be completed neatly. I've had countless children diagnosed as having the LD called agraphia (the inability to write neatly). With the application of consequences, however, both the inability to do homework and the inability to write neatly disappear.

You don't need to sit with your child night after night repeating the same questions and instructions to help him organize and complete his assignments, as recommended by other approaches. He can do it, and he will do it. IA-HM (ADD-ADHD) children can feign an inability to do the work with incredible theatrical effect. Set a reasonable time limit to get all homework neatly completed, and don't argue. Allow the consequences to motivate him; they will. Wrestling with difficult academic work is essential throughout life. It is in the figuring out, the deep concentration, the memorization, and the stress of making sense out of complex concepts that your child learns to learn. (Note that in psychology *learning to learn* is called *learning set.*)

Your child has to master working carefully and neatly, and he has to master deep concentration and focus. If you do the work for him, he will not master these cognitive skills. If you give him pills, he will not master these skills, because empirical evidence has shown that when you try to stop the pills, all gains in school work evaporate.

❏   6. *Column 6: Teacher's initials:* To avoid your child forging grades, have the teacher initial her grades. We don't like to think our kids would ever do something like that, but believe me, it's happened. Additional security measures will be offered shortly.

Tip: Structuring the Daily Routine

The DRC program works best if your child is permitted an hour and a half to two hours of free play after school each day. If yours is a two-working-parent or single-parent family, you may not be able to do this, but for others this is a plausible schedule. I believe that daily, after-school free play is healthy for developing social skills as well as for getting good physical exercise.

It also helps burn off excess energy after a hard day at school. However, free play has an additional importance: it becomes very important to children as part of their daily routine. Therefore, loss of free play can serve as a powerful daily consequence for failing to work and perform well in school. In other words, its loss can serve as a consequence for failure on the DRC.

STRUCTURE AND CONSEQUENCES

Grades on the DRC determine the daily consequences. Each day is considered a new start. Failure on one day allows a child a renewed try the next day. But continuous failures have a negative flip side, such as when negative consequences continue indefinitely or until the child decides to take school work and conduct seriously. The following are the recommended steps for enforcing the DRC Program.

❏   1. *Structuring the daily routine:*
   - Schedule free play after school each day.
   - Have your child come in from free play, wash, and then help set the dinner table. This gives her a sense of sharing family responsibilities.
   - Have dinner together as a family, at the dinner table. Most American families now eat dinner in front of the TV, often in separate rooms, which is a poor way to build family closeness.

- Have your child help with after-dinner clean-up as a way of improving responsibility.

- Have your child do homework after dinner. After looking at his assignments, allow a generous amount of time for finishing.

- After homework, allow one hour for watching TV. Monitor what your child watches; there's too much junk on TV.

- If time permits, require a half hour to one hour of personal, fun reading time. Other activities, such as drawing, should not be permitted as substitutes for reading.

- If time permits, allow drawing or playing quietly with toys.

- Set a regular bath time.

- Keep bedtime at exactly the same time every night. I believe children need structure to their daily routine.

- Read one or two bedtime stories to younger children.

- Stay by your child's bedside for a ten-minute chat.

Tip: The Nightly Chat

I can't emphasize enough the importance of a ten-minute chat as a nightly ritual. Don't preach and don't teach. Just engage in fun conversation; practice being a good listener. In this way you are growing close with your child as well as opening the lines of communication for when they will be needed later in life. Continue this nightly ritual throughout his entire life. When they are adults, sitting by the bed may not be appropriate; sitting in the living room serves as well. My boys come into my bedroom for our nightly chat, and they apparently love it. There have been times when they went to school sleepy the next day because our talk got particularly deep, and neither of us wanted to stop. I think the closeness and the values learned are occasionally worth the loss of a good night's sleep.

❑ 2. *Setting a criterion level:* Criterion level means the minimum expectation for *all* grades on your child's DRC. If the school psychologist's testing has indicated that your child is average for his intellectual level of functioning, the following are his DRC criterion responsibilities:

- S's or E's for all class performance and class conduct grades. Some schools use ABCDF; change the DRC to match your child's school preference.
- C's or better for all tests and quizzes returned.
- C's or better for all homework grades.

For children who score as "bright" on the intellectual test, higher criterion levels can be set, such as

- S's or E's for all class performance and class conduct grades. Use ABCDF on the DRC if they are used on your child's regular report card.
- B's or better for all tests and quizzes.
- B's or better for all homework grades.

Criterion levels are your choice; don't be excessively strict or too lenient.

☐ 3. *Permit no failures:* Absolutely no failures in any grades are permitted. *No grades below criterion level are acceptable—not one.*
☐ 4. *Enforce daily consequences:* A hierarchy of consequences follows. Make them stronger and stronger *if* your child continuously fails the DRC.

- *Level 1:* Loss of free play that day, for even one failure on the DRC.
- *Level 2:* If your child fails more than two days each week for two weeks, proceed with Level 2. This means loss of free play plus loss of watching TV.
- *Level 3:* If your child continues to fail two or more days each week, proceed with this level, which means that if your child has two days of failures during the week, he is grounded for the entire weekend. But grounding is much more severe than you may be used to because of the next rule.
- *Permit no substitutes:* In the CSP and the DRC program, loss of a reinforcer requires that no substitutes be allowed during the time period the child is supposed to have use of a reinforcer, whether it is an activity or an object.

If your child is grounded for a weekend, he is permitted to do nothing: no TV, no telephone, no toys, no reading, no going outside, no talking with you or anyone, nothing. If he uses anything, he completes his weekend in the time-out chair. Is this strict? Yes. But it is your child's choice. If he passes everything, he has free use of everything permitted in his daily routine. If he chooses to fail, he also chooses the negative consequences.

Rarely have I had a child go to the level of loss of a weekend. And even more rarely has a child lost more than two weekends before, miraculously, the diseases disappear and the child is passing everything.

THE BENEFITS OF THE DRC PROGRAM

By helping your child function well in school, you show him that he can function well anywhere in the world. This is a wonderful new realization because he probably believed he was sick and couldn't perform well on his own. I've seen children's smiles light up with genuinely earned pride when they discover they can pass all subjects and control their own conduct. They learn that they aren't sick and that they are just "a regular kid."

When a child is being well behaved and passing all subjects, even more positive things happen. A once-obnoxious child begins to be greeted by friendly faces and warm smiles. Adults, as well as other children, now like the person who was a dreaded terror. It may take a while for others to believe that these changes are permanent, but once they do believe it, your child will gain acceptance and be ever so much happier.

A True Story: David

Nine-year-old David was a super "H"—hyperactive and highly misbehaving. His parents reported that spending a day with David was like being on a high-speed roller coaster. He never seemed to stop. When playing out of doors he was always active; he loved to wrestle with other boys, ride his bike, roller blade, perform tricks on his skate board, and so forth. He loved playing video games, at times getting angry when he didn't win and at other times screaming with joy at defeating an imaginary enemy. He hated doing homework. Assignments were rarely completed and often appeared as if they had been dragged through the dirt during play. Most of the time he was a happy-go-lucky kid, but occasionally he'd have a nasty temper explosion, usually for not getting something he wanted. He was well liked by other children, and because of his excellence at sports, he was frequently chosen to be on teams. Getting him to bed on time was usually impossible. He preferred to stay up watching TV or playing with his toys. Admittedly, he was a likeable little boy, and it was clear that his parents adored him.

Poor school work seemed to be his main problem. He talked most all day at school. Other kids affectionately referred to him as "motor mouth." He was, indeed, very gregarious. He rarely finished assignments and never seemed to care. Daydreaming when he was supposed to be doing an assignment was typical. His grades were so poor that he was in danger of repeating the fifth grade.

The school psychologist and his teachers reported that his intellectual level of functioning was "very superior." His achievement test scores indicated that he was functioning several grade levels ahead in all skills, such as reading, math, and science. The teachers were mystified as to how he could be absorbing so much material when he never seemed to be paying attention.

When in my office he never sat still, continuously fidgeting, squirming, standing up, and often taking the pillows off the sofa.

He fit all the *DSM* criteria for ADHD.

David's parents saw little need to change his behaviors at home. They saw him as an energetic and happy-go-lucky little boy and did not wish to do anything that would destroy his wonderful spirit. I persuaded them that if he was placed on medication, as the school assessment team was recommending, his spirit would definitely be squelched. They had a difficult choice to make: either recognize that his high spiritedness was excessive and was disrupting the class as well as hurting his grades or enter into conflict with the school authorities. I convinced them that the CSP would radically improve behaviors that were interfering with doing well in school but would enhance behaviors that would help mobilize his enormous intellect. I gave them two weeks to make a decision.

When they returned they agreed to do the CSP, indicating that the persuading factor was knowing the children of several families with whom I had worked. Because of some initial reluctance, it took eight weeks to get David under control beyond the 90 percent mark on the Behavior Rating Scale. His parents were pleased because he retained his happy-go-lucky demeanor but used it in a more courteous manner. He was rough and tumble when it was appropriate, such as during free play, but well mannered when necessary, such as at the dinner table. His spiritedness wasn't at all stifled.

David's conduct and class performance at school, however, did not improve. After one month the DRC program was started. He lost free play. Two weeks later I was surprised because there were no signs of improvement. I thought that his loss of free play would be sufficient, but such was not the case. Next the loss of his nightly hour for watching TV was added. Again no improvement appeared on the DRC. A conference with his teacher confirmed that nothing had changed. The DRC was elevated to the next level, requiring full weekend grounding. His parents had a difficult time with this, believing the program was too restrictive. I encouraged them to enforce the consequences in order to make improvements happen as quickly as possible. He lost the first and second weekend. Finally, in week three, school performance, conduct, homework, and test grades dramatically improved. He began making A's and B's in all subjects and E's and S's in all his classes. Homework was neatly completed. He made such remarkable progress that by the end of the year, he was scheduled for placement in a class for the gifted for the next academic year.

I only saw David and his parents for a few visits during the following school year. He continued to do *extremely* well. Most impressive of all was that his end-of-the-year achievement testing scores placed him above the ninetieth percentile in all academic areas. And he is still a regular kid.

––––––

Now that your child is well behaved at home and at school and is doing well in his schoolwork, you have still more work to do. Conditions are now established for you to improve communications with your child and help her develop the strong values she'll need to sustain her through the long years of her education and in her future personal life. The next chapter will help with having more time together as a family, improving communications, teaching important values, and helping your child establish healthy peer relationships.

Part Three

BEYOND THE CAREGIVERS' SKILLS PROGRAM

II

TEACHING
IMPORTANT
VALUES

Now we're ready to go beyond the CSP. The CSP gets your IA-HM (ADD-ADHD) child's behaviors under control and begins activating his thinking and problem-solving abilities, but that is not the end of our process. Additional changes must take place so the gains your child makes are permanent.

Remember our discussion of the real familial and social causes of IA-HM (ADD-ADHD) in Chapter Three: the harried lifestyles, the frequent moves, the media, and so forth. Also recall the underlying cognitive patterns that result from this lifestyle: failing to think, hating school work and learning, hating reading, and not respecting authority figures. The CSP has helped your child improve her respect for authority, mostly for you and for teachers, and has helped activate her cognitions, thus making her aware and responsible for her behaviors. She is now more vigilant and respectful of the impact of her behavior on others. But still more is needed.

In Chapter Three I also discussed parents who unintentionally fail to give children sufficient time and attention to meet their nurturance needs and teach them important values. In this chapter I offer suggestions to help you have more time for your child, improve family closeness, and help teach your child the very important values of loving learning, loving reading, and having healthier peer relationships. The following solutions are presented:

- Solution One: Improving time and communication while reducing stress

- Solution Two: Helping your IA-HM (ADD-ADHD) child love learning

- Solution Three: Helping your IA-HM (ADD-ADHD) child love reading

- Solution Four: Helping your IA-HM (ADD-ADHD) child have better peer relationships

SOLUTION ONE: IMPROVING TIME AND COMMUNICATION WHILE REDUCING STRESS

The CSP requires that you work with your child. It is essential that you have sufficient time to help him change. Wouldn't it be a lot easier if you gave your child a pill every day and brought him to a therapist's office once each week for a one-hour session? Indeed, for you that would simplify things. But it would not produce the real changes you want for your child.

One-hour weekly sessions produce few or no changes in ADD-ADHD (IA-HM) children. Therapists are not possessed with magical powers. They would be no more effective than you would be in convincing your child to change. And the pills, as we have discussed at length, would only constrain and repress your child's behavior. Pills teach nothing, and each time you try to stop the pills, all the problem behaviors and inattention return. Remember: pills are the least healthy solution. For the CSP to work and for you to teach values, you will need to put in substantial time, energy, and effort.

"But Dr. Stein, I don't have any time for my child. I can barely make it through a day, and when I get home from work I'm exhausted." I know you are. I understand. I feel the same way myself. However, there are solutions to your dilemma. There are ways both you and your child can be winners. In this chapter I suggest ten steps you can take to have more time with your child, improve closeness, and develop better parent-child communication. You will have the time required to make the CSP work and reduce many of the stresses that have been controlling your life and your child's life.

Having a Close and Loving Relationship

The CSP program is only a beginning. It gets the ADD-ADHD (IA-HM) completely under control to resume the loving and close relationship you once had. The obnoxious behaviors that sometimes led you to feel that you couldn't stand your own child should now be gone; so too should any guilt you may be experiencing. Feelings of warmth and love are probably returning. You and your child can once again bond. Under these conditions you can help change your child's values, which is the key to making life-long changes.

Making Changes

It would be unreasonable to expect that you can make all of the suggested changes. But place a check mark in the boxes before those changes you think you can make.

❑ 1. *Have breakfast with your child every morning.* "What!" you say. "There's no time in the morning."
Here's how it's done. You and your child must awaken fifteen or twenty minutes earlier in order to have breakfast together at the kitchen table. This starts the day with family time and with warmth and caring. Be cheery, and keep the conversation light. Whatever you do, *"Don't preach and don't teach."* Don't make breakfast a repressive ordeal for your child.

❑ 2. *Have dinner together as a family.* Do not eat dinner in front of the TV. Our goal is family unity. Again, keep the conversation light.

❑ 3. *Turn off the TV one hour each night and read together.* Typically, American families adjourn to separate rooms, thus allowing each family member to watch his or her favorite shows. If the family remains in the same room, bonding rarely occurs because everyone sits unconnected in front of the TV like parallel zombies.

Are you a reader? Do you need some inner peace? Or are you a TV junkie? You are a role model for your child. What he observes you doing are the behaviors he is likely to adopt. Is reading an activity you can make happen for you and your child for at least one hour each evening?

❑ 4. *Start a nightly ritual of sitting by your child's bed to chat.* Our goal is for your child to want to talk with you. It is through years of gentle and soft conversations that your child will internalize your values. An excellent time for these quiet talks is at bedtime. Can you perform this as a nightly ritual?

❑   5. *Honor your family's day of weekly rest and closeness.* I remember when many cities in the United States honored blue laws. On Sunday all businesses were closed except pharmacies and gas stations. The world seemed to come to a standstill. Families usually went to church or synagogue and returned home to a wonderful meal and warm family time together. It saddens me that such days are gone. Hustling seven days a week to get chores done is commonplace. We don't rest anymore. This isn't good for our children, and it isn't good for us. It is within our power to reestablish our Sabbath, whether Saturday or Sunday, as a day of renewal. And if you are not a religious family and don't attend regular worship, you can take a day off every week as a family habit.

The stores may remain open, but we need not honor them. If we are diligent, we can complete most of our chores during the week; if all of them aren't done, well, so what? Even God rested on the seventh day.

❑   6. *If you are a two-parent family, is it possible for one of you to quit work to become a full-time parent?* Don't go ballistic. Later in this chapter I'll demonstrate that it may actually be better financially for one parent to stay home. You may be losing money by both of you working. If you are both career-oriented or if you're a single parent, this may not be an option. But if you are like 80 percent of people who are employed, you may be working at a job you don't really like. There are many benefits when one of you stays home, such as having more disposable cash, less stress, a cleaner home, more home-cooked meals, and, most important, *more time for your child.* Don't answer this question until you complete the exercise on budgeting.

❑   7. *Reduce the number of organized sports and activities in which your child participates.* Too many of our children participate in too many activities. ADD-ADHD (IA-HM) children are wound-up machines, in good measure because they are overprogrammed. They don't have stress-free time to just be kids. Free play is important for the physical, social, and emotional development of children.

❑ 8. *Reduce the number of community-related activities in which you participate.* Many of us try to impose a family model based on conditions as they were years ago. When one person worked and the other stayed home, there was ample time to contribute time and energy to the church and community. Today things are very different. For families in which both spouses work or for single parents, participation in these activities may be robbing a child of much-needed time and attention. Devotion to such services is important, but if it leaves us with little time for our children, then it is a mistake. We can't do everything, and our children must come first. Consider whether participation in these additional activities leaves you more tired and irritable and thus impairs your interactions with your child.

❑ 9. *Stop moving and stabilize your family's life.* Has moving from place to place disrupted the life of your family? Was moving unavoidable? "Unavoidable" does *not* include moving for promotions. More and more executives are refusing to move for the sake of their families, and I applaud them. Recall what I discussed earlier about the impact of moving on your child's life, including loss of friends, the need to start over as the new kid in a new school, and loss of the extended family. Security and stability are important to children. Our modern world is overstressed enough; moving only multiplies the exceptional pressures on a child. This is not something pills can fix.

❑ 10. *Have lots of fun together as a family.* Take time, at least once a month, to do fun family activities. Go to a concert or theater. Take camping trips. Go hiking. Take educational excursions to museums. Visit historical sites. Attend sporting events. Take a day to raft slowly down a winding river. Make a list of other activities you can do as a family, and place check marks next to those you can be certain to do. Then do them.

If you practice most of these steps, you will build a close and loving relationship with your child. It is only in this way that you will exert a positive influence over the values she adopts. If your relationship is predominantly negative, consisting mostly of arguments, harsh remarks, and anger, don't expect to influence your child's value system. You and your child can have it all: fun, closeness, stability, love, calmness, and emotional health. Your child doesn't have a disease. With the CSP we can eliminate ADD-ADHD (IA-HM) behaviors, and with the suggestions in this chapter you can start the process of preventing your child from returning to inappropriate behaviors.

THE POSSIBILITY OF QUITTING WORK

Earlier I mentioned the possibility of one parent quitting his or her job in order to devote more time and attention to the needs of a child. If you're a single parent or if both of you are working, then it is likely that your child attends day care. It is not unusual for children to be placed in day care a few weeks after birth. Preschool children often spend twelve or more hours each day at a day care facility.

Day Care and IA-HM (ADD-ADHD)

Most day care workers are not college graduates. It's becoming fashionable to call them teachers, but they aren't. Some seem more like unarmed guards. *Chaos, pandemonium, confusion,* and *hell* are only a few of the descriptive words I can conjure up for some day care facilities. There are some very conscientious and sensitive facilities out there, but even the best of them can't give kids the attention and nurturance they need. It saddens me that too many of our children are raised in such environments.

Has day care significantly contributed to the emergence over the past twenty years of so many inattentive and misbehaving children, whom we arbitrarily call ADD-ADHD? Yes, very likely. Do a child's nurturance needs get sufficiently met in day care? Not likely. Is this an environment in which to develop a serene temperament? Not always. Are proper behaviors taught in such a place? Not often. Do day care personnel contribute significantly to children developing a healthy value system? Not frequently. Too many parents inadvertently impose these conditions on children, convince them they are diseased, and then control them with powerful chemicals. Am I the only one who sees something terribly wrong with this picture?

In my discussions with students I ask what their intentions are about having children. Is day care what they want for their infants and toddlers? I often quote to them something the actress Bette Davis once said: "There are three parts to my life—my marriage, my career, and my children. I can only handle two." College students are typically on their way toward careers, and I believe that this is an issue with which they must come to terms. I ask them to consider what is best for the children.

Improvement in Cash Flow

Not only may it be possible for one parent to stay home to devote full time to raising a child, but it may actually be financially advantageous. If you are living in a two-parent home, I suggest that both of you carefully fill out the following budget twice—first as your budget currently is and second as what you think your budget could be if one of you stays home and makes the recommended lifestyle changes. To get a clear picture calculate weekly expenses for each item, and then multiply by 50 (that's subtracting two weeks of vacation) for yearly amounts.

Items	Mom	Dad
All yearly job-related expenses for two cars:		
• Gas to get to and from work	$_____	$_____
• Tolls	$_____	$_____
• Depreciation of each car's value ($.40 per mile)	$_____	$_____
• Parking fees	$_____	$_____
• Car repairs	$_____	$_____
• Clothing expenses related to work	$_____	$_____
Extra food expenses because of two jobs, including fast food purchases, amounts for children, and children's lunches	$_____	$_____
Total income less job-related expenses:	$_____	$_____
Add the savings you could realize if one person stays home and does the following:		
• Plans and prepares meals	$_____	$_____
• Clips grocery coupons (possibly up to $30.00 per week)	$_____	$_____
• Packs brown-bag lunches or serves home lunches	$_____	$_____
• Keeps children and avoids day care expenses	$_____	$_____

Items	Mom	Dad
Add the income you might generate if one of you worked from home:		
• Providing day care for a few children approximately $80.00 per week per child	$_____	$_____
• Doing a computer-based job	$_____	$_____
• Conducting a business	$_____	$_____
Add tax deductions for working from your home:		
• Food purchases if you're providing day care	$_____	$_____
• Mortgage deduction equal to % of square footage of house used for your business	$_____	$_____
• Equipment like play equipment, toys, computer, TV, office equipment (including supplies)	$_____	$_____
• Use of your car for business purposes	$_____	$_____
Add tax savings for reduced cash income	$_____	$_____
Subtract approximate expenses for taking time off to care for sick children	$_____	$_____
Net Income	$_____	$_____

There is one more important question: Can you "downsize" your lifestyle? Can you live in a smaller house, drive smaller cars, and dress less expensively in order for one of you to be home for the children?

It may be scary to give up a regular paycheck, but after doing this exercise it may be apparent that one parent staying home can considerably improve your cash flow. Consider the reductions simply in daily stresses by one person staying home: a cleaner house, wonderful home-cooked meals, not rushing to go shopping, and, most important, being able to give your child more individual time and attention.

SOLUTION TWO: HELPING YOUR IA-HM (ADD-ADHD) CHILD LOVE LEARNING

There are two parts to the diagnosis of IA-HM (ADD-ADHD): (1) being inattentive and (2) being hyperactive or highly misbehaving. The CSP has taken care of the second (hyperactive) part and partially taken care of the first. It has helped your child respect your authority and that of others. To improve attention even more, a child must internalize two values: (1) the love of learning and (2) the love of reading. Then the inattentiveness component will completely disappear. The so-called disease will evaporate. This has happened with hundreds of children, and it will also happen with yours. Count on it.

SEVEN STEPS TO HELPING YOUR IA-HM (ADD-ADHD) CHILD LOVE LEARNING

There are seven steps you can take to help your child love learning. Almost without fail every IA-HM (ADD-ADHD) child I have interviewed has flatly stated that he or she *hates* schoolwork and learning. Learning in school is not easy; it is hard work. A child must sit in an uncomfortable chair for six or more hours each day while painstakingly attending to material that is hard to master and often, quite frankly, boring. Learning in school requires strong motivation. To succeed, children must be highly motivated in two ways:

1. They must love the learning process itself.

2. They must be goal- or future-oriented.

Because of my own love for learning it saddens me that so many children hate school work. Remember that hating school work is a common characteristic of children labeled as IA-HM (ADD-ADHD). This negative attitude is both curable and preventable if you take the following steps:

❑ 1. *Assess your own beliefs about education and learning.* What message do you project to your child? Is your belief, "Get a good education to get a good job?" Are you therefore projecting a covert message that school is something you must tolerate as a roadblock along the journey to what you really value—a good income? If such is your belief, then as a role model you are teaching that learning is not fun and that the journey through years of education is to be considered painful. If you want your child to love her education, then you must change first. It is not fair to expect your child to perform well in school and to care about school if you don't.

❑ 2. At least once each month, have a family activity day when everyone visits educational sites such as museums and historical places. These enriching trips are not just informational; they also convey your love for learning while enhancing family closeness. Doing these activities helps form warm family memories, which become associated with learning activities. Learning, developing a love for learning, and loving each other as a family—all in one nicely wrapped package. It doesn't get much better than this.

A True Story: My Kids and I in New York

Two years ago during the Christmas holidays, my sons, Alex and Kevin, and I took a trip to New York City. We had a wonderful time visiting many exciting places, such as the World Trade Center (note: this was written before our sad events), museums, and the Staten Island ferry. All of these sites, by the way, were inexpensive. While at the American Museum of Natural History, we visited the Early American exhibits. I asked the boys to look around and think of all the people and the types of careers necessary to create the exhibits. The list grew long and included archeologists, biologists, anthropologists, historians, and so on. We talked about the work these people did and what their daily routines must be like. We talked about careers that involved climbing mountains, exploring forests, digging in the earth, diving in the oceans, and exploring caves. The boys became animated with excitement. We were all learning, having fun, and enjoying family time. I deeply believe that memories such as these create a love for learning, a love for travel, a love for family, as well as reflections on what they might wish to do with their lives.

❑ 3. *Make learning about nature important and fun.* Take trips to scenic places. Go camping and teach your child camping skills. Go day hiking. Get up early to watch the sun rise. Buy a telescope and scan the heavens. The joys of nature are endless, and so too is learning about nature.

❑ 4. *Visit college campuses.* Free tours can easily be arranged. Colleges want you and your child to visit. It may mean future business for them. For many children college is an abstract concept. Take your kids to visit different campuses to make college more real to them. Most campuses are beautiful. Falling in love with a particular campus can provide a strong incentive to help your child remain focused on his schoolwork. College tour guides often recount fascinating tales about the college's history and famous graduates. They also usually teach about the school's architecture. These trips are free, fun, and informative.

❏ 5. *Expand your child's love for all types of music*. Children can continue enjoying their favorite types of music while developing an appreciation for a wider variety. The best way to accomplish this is to take your child to live concerts. Many communities have free summer concerts. Have your child sample all types of live music: rock, pop, classical, jazz, blue-grass, country, Latin, blues, and so on. Nearby colleges often perform marvelous concerts for very low prices.

❏ 6. *Take your child to plays*. Live theater is a wonderful treat for children. Most communities have children's theaters, and as your children get older they can come with you to more adult performances. This is a great way to expand entertainment beyond junk TV. My son Alex is passionate about reading plays. He loves the works of Sam Shepard, Neil Simon, Thornton Wilder, Arthur Miller, and many others. His love began by attending community children's productions. Most communities have free outdoor summer presentations. Go as a family. Pack a picnic. Have a great time.

❏ 7. *Show a continuing active and enthusiastic interest in your child's school work*. Ask her daily about school. If you listen well, your child will want to share her school experiences with you. If you have a close and loving relationship, she'll want to please you. If her education is important to you, it will become important to her.

If you've implemented Solutions One and Two, you are well on your way to eliminating your child's IA-HM (ADD-ADHD) cognitive and behavioral habits. With each step you'll become more and more convinced that IA-HM (ADD-ADHD) are not diseases. Next we'll move closer to our goal of a complete "cure" by working on another solution: helping your child love reading.

SOLUTION THREE: HELPING YOUR IA-HM (ADD-ADHD) CHILD LOVE READING

A few IA-HM (ADD-ADHD) children enjoy reading; most don't. The love of reading helps to reduce IA-HM (ADD-ADHD) behavioral and cognitive patterns. Nevertheless this is an extremely important aspect of changing your child's habits. Good reading skills are essential for making good grades. Poor grades are one of the main reasons these children are referred for treatment.

Don't despair if in the past you've tried unsuccessfully to get your child to become a reader. Our goal is to get your child to *want* to read. You can actually get your child to *love reading*.

Two elements are required if children are to become good readers: *mechanics* and *practice*. Mechanics (reading skills) are usually well taught in school, but schools often fail to inspire children to practice. Many educators, including myself, believe that the best way to improve reading skills is to read. Practice is sometimes called experiential reading. To succeed at this it is crucial to get children motivated to *want* to read.

Although learning the mechanics of reading skills such as phonics or word attack skills is important, practice is far more important. It is here that some of the reading assignments teachers make can be counterproductive; they can contribute to children disliking—even hating—to read.

Before I discuss how you can help your child love reading, here are some things *not* to do. Your school might be doing these things, but they should be avoided:

- *Giving points and rewards.* Schools often provide extensive reading lists; children can accumulate points for each book they read. A point system like this is actually a form of token economy. By earning points for reading, prizes can be purchased when enough points are accumulated. As a life-long educator I find that under these conditions, children *act* as if they are reading when all they are doing is rushing through the books to earn prizes. This doesn't allow them to get into the content. I'm also not crazy about paying children for a behavior that should be intrinsically rewarding. Under proper conditions reading can be lots of fun, and there's no need to reinforce the act. What value do we teach children when they associate getting paid with reading? Reading should be for reading's sake alone.

- *Composing elite reading lists.* School reading lists are often composed of books that are considered classics or educationally important. But to the children they are often difficult and dull. Having reviewed many of these books, I often find them to be complex and difficult to read or just plain inappropriate for many kids who have a wide variety of interests. Our children have different personalities and levels of skill. Of course some books are worth reading for most everyone, but kids need to have their own customized reading lists, with books that are appropriate for their special temperaments, experience, tastes, and passions.

To me the goal should be for a child to be so deeply immersed in a book that he wouldn't hear a firecracker go off in the next room. You want to see your child unable to put a book down rather than unwilling to pick it up. Books on a list should be relatively easy, with choices that can capture children's imaginations. Help eliminate the elitism underlying the selections. Children will read more complex books when their tastes and skills are sufficiently advanced, and this will happen naturally if only we can get them to want to read, read, read.

• *Insisting on following boring summer reading lists.* Summers are special for children. They are times for reckless abandonment. For children, summers should be a time for freedom and fun. And reading can and should perpetuate such delightful feelings. Instead children are often given reading lists filled with the same problems we just discussed. The selections are mostly elitist, boring, complex, and dull. What normal, healthy kid wants to pick up a book in the middle of summer that dampens her fun and spirits? This doesn't have to be. When I take my children to a local bookstore, the woman in charge of the young people's section always asks them what topics they enjoy or what authors they have enjoyed in the past. She'll then direct them to several possibilities. If one of my sons selects a book, I'll then test him by having him read a few randomly selected paragraphs. If he becomes bored or trips over every other word, I'll request that we try a different selection. We continue this process until we leave with several books for each of the boys.

Whenever the boys and I don't like the teacher's selections, I ask her for permission to make substitutions. She usually cheerfully complies. Then she's happy, I'm happy, and most important, the boys are happy. They can look forward to taking time out of their busy summer activities for some quiet reading. I love to observe them during a wonderful Virginia summer rain, curled up with a great book, in utter peace and bliss. They look so content that my heart fills with joy. This is what reading should do for children. It should give them times of bliss and serenity. It should feel good.

DETECTING READING PROBLEMS

Good reading skills are honed and sharpened by the daily practice of reading. Can you get your child to *want* to read each and every day? Definitely, yes! You can get your child to read with the same intensity he gives to video games and television. Follow the steps I'll outline, and there is an excellent chance your child will truly *love reading*.

Before you get started, I have one caution. Sometimes undetected problems may be present that can interfere with your child's ability to read well. If these problems continue undetected, your child will be frustrated by his inability to understand what he has read. He won't enjoy reading, and he won't be motivated to read. Detecting and clearing up these problems is crucial.

Check the box to be certain you have properly ruled out each potential problem:

❑   1. *Know your child's current reading level.* Reading cannot become fun if you are selecting material that is too difficult. In many school districts skill-evaluation testing is done at the beginning and end of each academic year. Most reading scores are expressed by reading grade level. For example, a score of 4.7 means that a child is reading at the fourth grade, seventh-month level. If the score were for a child in the third grade, she would be considerably advanced, whereas a child in the fifth grade would be a bit behind. Sometimes scores are represented as percentiles. The fiftieth percentile represents a score that is in the exact middle for a child's grade and age group; a score in the thirty-fifth percentile is below average, and a seventieth percentile is above average. Scores are sometimes camouflaged with what are called standard scores. Usually you will receive a written explanation to help understand the score, but these can be confusing. Have your child's teacher help you understand them.

❑   2. *Have your child's vision and hearing checked yearly by a qualified specialist.* It is not unusual for these problems to remain undetected, and they can certainly interfere with reading mastery.

❑   3. *Check for undetected learning disabilities (LDs).* Teachers are trained to pick up potential waning signs, but sometimes LDs can slip past even the most astute teacher. If your child is not reading well, make an official request to have the school psychologist or other qualified person in the community have her tested. As I stated earlier, IA-HM (ADD-ADHD) and LDs often occur simultaneously, simply because the child wasn't paying attention when fundamental skills in a particular subject were being taught. LDs involve a deficit in one or two subject areas when a child's overall intellectual functioning is normal or above normal. It is difficult to advance in any subject if the fundamentals are not well learned, and once a child falls behind, without special tutoring she may not be able to catch up. On rare occasions perceptual problems may interfere with the learning process, and these are very hard to detect. Special tutoring involves relearning the fundamentals by multisensory teaching methods, which I mentioned elsewhere.

❑ 4. *Check to see if your child may be an undetected slow learner.* This means that a child's intellectual level of functioning may be sufficiently below grade level to make it difficult for him to keep pace with his class in reading and probably with all subjects. Such a child can make excellent progress in small self-paced classes. With the right selection of reading material, reading can become fun for him, too. A school psychologist, mental health professional, or private psychologist can perform the necessary evaluation.

One additional point: if a child has an exceptionally high intelligence, he may bored with work that is too easy and unchallenging. This too can underlie the big ADD-ADHD (IA-HM) problems.

Any one of these problems can interfere with reading and contribute to attention problems as well. It is difficult to maintain attention when a child doesn't understand what is going on. And when a child isn't paying attention and is bored, it's easy for him to start misbehaving. Then the "H" gets added to the "ADD" part of the diagnosis.

TWELVE STEPS TO HELP YOUR CHILD LOVE READING

Check each step that you implement:

❑ 1. *Read to younger children at bedtime.* Children younger than age eight love to be read to; children eight and older usually consider this to be babyish. For younger children this nightly ritual has considerable importance.

Scientists know that younger children's brains are at their peak for learning language. As children grow older this ability seems to decline. Traditionally, schools teach languages at about the seventh grade when this receptive ability has considerably diminished. But some school districts now teach two foreign languages starting in the first grade, when the children seem to learn the languages effortlessly. The important point is that your child's brain is receptive to language very early in life, and by reading to him you increase and enhance his auditory vocabulary. This is excellent preparation for sight reading. In addition, a child develops an association between the written word and the magical fantasies that form in his mind. He also associates the reading of a book with the warmth and security of a close parent.

Pay careful attention to the types of stories he loves, such as adventure, sports, funny, or fairy tales. Try to choose the themes he loves most. When selecting stories to read to your child, try to choose ones that are at or above his current reading level, not at grade level. In this way you'll be introducing more advanced auditory vocabulary, which helps with word attack skills for sight reading. Try not to select too advanced materials or you'll be so busy explaining new words that the story line will be lost, and this defeats the purpose: making this nightly ritual fun.

If your child wants you to read a particular story every night, do it. But to expand his repertoire, require that the favorite book be followed by a new story. Most children do not want to go to sleep right away, so he'll usually see this as a way to outsmart you.

❑ 2. *Make reading easy.* When selecting materials for your child to read on her own, choose books that are from her current level to lower levels. This reduces tripping over too many words and allows her to become immersed in the story content. Getting her to become deeply wrapped up in a story is our goal. If she can't put the book down or can't wait until she can pick her book up to find out what's going to happen next, then you'll know that reading is becoming fun for your child.

To make certain that your child is choosing books with an appropriate level of difficulty, open a chosen book to any random page and have your child read a paragraph, then repeat this a second time. If your child is frequently tripping over words, make a different choice. To avoid embarrassing your child, emphasize that you want him to have fun and that choosing a too-difficult book destroys getting into the story, which is what is most important.

❑ 3. *Allow bedtime reading.* Instead of engaging in a nightly battle with a child who doesn't want to go to sleep on time, allow him to stay up an extra thirty minutes for reading. No other activity, such as drawing or playing with a toy, is permitted. It's reading only. Bedtime reading is an activity that you want to become habitual. Younger readers may substitute magazines or picture books. If you later peek in his room and he's under the blanket reading by flashlight, back out quietly and smile. It's working.

❑ 4. *Frequent the library.* The library should be a familiar and comfortable place, and this only happens with frequent visits. Make it a point to visit the library with your child at least every two weeks. Select books to read to her, and for her to read, and be certain to follow the recommended guidelines made earlier for selecting the books.

❑ 5. *Subscribe to several children's magazines in your child's name.* Children love to receive mail. If you subscribe to several children's magazines in your child's name, you'll soon discover that every day he'll race you to be first to the mailbox. Within seconds he'll be curled up with the latest issue, which is what you're trying to achieve.

❑ 6. *Allow comic books, but choose carefully.* A long-time myth has existed that comic books are bad for reading. That's false. Comics can be a lot of fun, but choose carefully; some are too violent or are risqué. If only I'd saved the comics I had as a kid, I'd be rich! Be prepared for how expensive comics are now. You may be shocked.

❑ 7. *Make reading a family activity.* Americans watch too much TV. Can you turn the TV off for one hour each evening for family reading time? If you're not a habitual reader, try reading the newspaper or a magazine—but read. You are a role model for your child. If he sees you being a couch potato, then that is what he will do. Reading together as a family stimulates closeness and warmth. When the TV is on everyone sits in parallel and doesn't connect. Can you at least allow this one hour for reading? Often during this time family conversations start, again setting the stage for family closeness.

❑ 8. *Build a small book collection for your child.* I worship books, and so do most of my colleagues. Books should be revered, and you can help your child develop this deep value by starting his or her small collection. Of course, for some families the expense may be prohibitive, but if it is within with your budget, build your child's library. Buy paperbacks and secondhand books at used-book stores, flea markets, and garage sales. You can often find terrific bargains. Take your child with you; these hunting excursions can be fun. Make collecting books a special source of fun and pride.

❑ 9. *Show your interest in her reading.* More parents are passive in the raising of their children than I care to think about. They seem to operate under a misguided philosophy that children can raise themselves. They show little concern about guiding the direction of their children's lives. This often shows up in school work. They seem to believe that the teachers will fulfill all their children's needs. Child development requires a lot of effort and planning. This is especially true for developing a love for the written word. It is essential that parents take an active interest in their child's reading. Every day inquire, ask questions, and show your enthusiasm. Listen carefully to what your child tells you, and ask him to tell you more. Your interest will motivate him.

❑ 10. *Fill your home with an abundance of reading material.* Are you aware of the automatic habit of picking up and reading a magazine in your doctor's office or at the hair salon? Why not do this for your child at home? Leave it out, and she'll pick it up and read it.

❑ 11. *Have a special reading place.* Children often love having a part of the house they can think of as their special place. With a little thought this place can be conducive to reading. It can be an overstuffed chair, a beanbag, or a pile of large pillows. Ask your child what she might like, and then try to make it so. Having a cozy place of her own can help her want to read.

❑ 12. *Be sneaky.* Here's a little secret I use. Have you ever noticed that sometimes when you're talking to another adult, it seems that your child isn't listening? Well, he is! I'm certain you've been amazed months later by his recalling a conversation you had when you thought he wasn't listening. Kids hear everything! When you are with another adult and your child is within earshot, deliberately discuss your pride in her reading. Let your child accidentally overhear your enthusiasm. This may be sneaky, but it sure is powerful as a motivator.

Remember: the child who loves reading and learning *and* respects authority doesn't *ever* become IA-HM (ADD-ADHD). And you can take that to the bank! You'll need to when he goes to college.

SOLUTION FOUR: HELPING YOUR IA-HM (ADD-ADHD) CHILD HAVE BETTER PEER RELATIONSHIPS

Few parents think about how their children develop friendships. Other children with whom your child is close can have a major impact on his values. Friends gain more and more influence as your child approaches the teen years.

If your child's friends don't like school, chances are neither will your child. Too many children come from families whose parents care little about education, which is the attitude their children will adopt. The best way to control who your child becomes friends with is to enroll your child in Sunday school, special after-school programs, Boy Scouts, sports, or other activities that attract good kids. Make certain you know the children and their parents. Don't overdo the number of activities. Allow the bonding to happen gradually.

The best child and teen programs that are sponsored by houses of worship, the Girl Scouts and Boy Scouts, the YMCA, or other community organizations are designed to offer fun alternatives *every weekend*. Having parties and lock-ins, bowling, swimming, snow skiing, water skiing, dancing, ice skating, and roller blading are activities churches should be providing. My formula is this:

Fun + Fellowship = Spirituality

In a wholesome atmosphere of fun and fellowship, spiritual values will eventually take on importance. Peers with strong values, developed from families invested in teaching these values, are the kind of friends you want your child to have. Slowly their values will become important to your child. Help make this happen.

In the next and final chapter I discuss specific ways to avoid creating an IA-HM (ADD-ADHD) child if you don't already have one. And I try to clear up a misconception some readers might have: that I'm blaming parents when they have such a child. I'm certainly not doing that, and I explain why in

Chapter Twelve. There's plenty of blame to go around; I've already mentioned many of the culprits, including psychologists and drug companies. The last I'll mention are the politicians responsible for creating educational systems in which many children can't function normally.

12

PREVENTING THE CREATION OF AN IA-HM (ADD-ADHD) CHILD

If IA-HM (ADD-ADHD) were truly diseases, there wouldn't be a thing you or I or anyone could do to prevent their onset. Now that you've completed working with your child, you probably realize that. You may now be convinced that you and many other parents have been had.

WHY I DON'T BLAME PARENTS

Sometimes parents interpret what I have to say as blaming parents. I'm not. I do blame politicians. I'll explain my reasons for both, but here's why I don't blame parents:

1. *Parents had little control over the way our economic system has affected our home lives.* Twenty years ago no one foresaw how out of control our lives would become. No one predicted the overwhelming avalanche of daily hassles we face or that it would take two working people to afford the American dream of having children, a nice house, and two cars. At some point the whole thing got out of control.

2. *I doubt that anyone understood how reliant we would become on day care to raise our children.* Most people want children, and most believed they could do

it all: have children, work, maintain a house. It's not working out that way, is it? No one predicted that the divorce rate would skyrocket to 50 percent and that 50 percent of all children would be raised by single working parents who have no choice but to rely on day care.

3. *No one foresaw that conditions in the classroom would create a difficult learning environment:* our overcrowded classrooms and the reduction of resources for fun courses such as music, art, and physical education. Politicians didn't foresee that their policies would create curricula that overemphasize hardcore academic courses, making learning boring and turning off so many children to learning.

4. *No one taught us how to be skilled at the art of parenting.* We began parenthood without a clue about how to raise children. And until now no one came up with answers for getting out-of-control children back under control.

5. *Parents have been victims of a massive campaign to sell drugs.* Economics has obliterated integrity in psychiatry and psychology. To pull this campaign off, the following had to take place:

- *Psychologists and psychiatrists had to convince the public that inattentive and highly misbehaving children were the victims of diseases.*
- *Psychologists and psychiatrists had to convince the public that medications (I prefer the term "drugs") were the only real solution.*
- *Psychologists had to blindly accept an unproven disease theory and therefore fail to develop effective parent-training models to remedy the problem.*
- *Pharmaceutical companies had to recruit researchers, educators, psychologists, and psychiatrists to participate in this disease-drug campaign, making many of them rich in the process.* As Elliot Valenstein (1998), Richard DeGrandpre (1999), and Steve Baldwin and Rebecca Anderson (2000) point out; and as presented at the New York Ritalin Litigation Conference; and as many concerned people have told me directly, the seeding of money has been key. Drug companies have provided money for expensive speaking engagements, money to make professional journals profitable, money that is placed directly in professional organization treasuries, money to attend conferences (sometimes in exotic places), money merely to attend a presentation for psychiatric drugs, money to sit on the boards of pharmaceutical companies, and money for consulting

work—all in unbelievable amounts. Drug companies have bought and are still buying the integrity of too many psychologists and psychiatrists.

• *Practicing psychologists, psychiatrists, and physicians had to accept junk research as gospel.* Worse are those who knew it was junk and did nothing about it.State and national ethics committees had to ignore and do nothing about the junk research designed for the drugging of millions of children.

• *The American Medical Association has stood by during psychiatry's and psychology's campaign for the unnecessary drugging of children.* How much will it take for this venerable professional institution to take a proper moral stand?

• *TV media moguls, interested in ratings and the ever-popular bulwark of money, have had to allow garbage shows to target the hours children most watch.* They've contributed to airing role models who teach a hostility for education and a disrespect for authority. Has everybody in business stopped caring about our children!?

No, I don't blame parents—especially not in the face of such difficult circumstances.

WHAT PARENTS CAN DO

Following are a list of practices that can help you, as an enlightened parent, prevent your child from either becoming ADD-ADHD or returning to IA-HM (ADD-ADHD) cognitive and behavioral practices:

• *Don't send your child to day care unless it is absolutely necessary.*

• *If you're in a two-parent home, one of you stay home as a full-time parent.* Can one of you stop working? Children need a full-time parent for guidance and nurturing.

• *Quit yelling and screaming at your child.* This only trains him to tune you out and enhances inattentiveness.

• *Stop regularly spanking or hitting your child.* This only contributes to his anxiety and resentment. Follow the guidelines presented earlier for time out and spanking.

- *Stop giving in and reinforcing verbal manipulations such as when your child cries "poor me," nags, and interrupts.*

- *Be firm with your child.* Use the CSP.

- *Be consistent at the art and science of parenting.* Now you know the CSP, and there are no excuses. You can do it well.

- *Don't do everything for your child.* Teach her skills and family responsibilities, and then make her do them. Help her be independent.

- *Stop sitting with him during homework.* He can do it on his own. Doing it for him will not help.

- *Stop treating her as if she were handicapped.* Make her responsible for her behavior and for hard work.

- *Don't allow him to watch junk TV.* Don't allow him to watch too much of any TV, because it encourages passivity and mindlessness if too many hours a day are spent zoned out in front of the tube.

- *Don't remind him of everything he should be doing.* Simply invoke the consequences and require that he do what he's supposed to. Train him to think actively and remember.

- *Stop warning her.* Let the consequences require that she remember. She can.

- *Praise him when he does something right.*

- *Know who your child's friends are.* Help him connect with healthy and strong-valued peers.

- *Make education and a love for learning important values.*

- *Help him love reading.* Take all the necessary steps to make reading important to him.

- *Stop letting him get by with testing behaviors.* Use time out at the mere hint of misbehavior.

- *Stop allowing him to defy you.* Be firm; you now have the CSP as your guide.

- *Help end the mischief surrounding IA-HM (ADD-ADHD).* Be proactive and help educate two families you know that there is a better way. If all of you do this, we will have healthier, happier, and well-behaved children.

WHY I BLAME POLITICS

Politics plays a large part in creating the problems in America's system of education. Something is terribly wrong with the schools themselves, and I see politicians as deserving a major part of the blame. Many of them express concern publicly that school children in the United States are academically behind children from other countries. They often cite France, Germany, Spain, and Japan as leaders in education. Many even campaign on the cliché "back to basics," which means an ever-increasing length of the academic day of reading, writing, and mathematics and less and less emphasis on fun things such as music, art, physical education, free play, and healthy exercise. Consequently the school day is becoming increasingly dull, dull, dull!

Don't confuse basics with fundamentals. The term *basics* refers to subjects; *fundamentals* refers to skills. Skills can be taught in more fun and inventive ways by incorporating them in the arts, music, and physical health activities. Instead politicians are emphasizing more and more school hours focused on academic subjects.

Another result of political posturing has been to accelerate school subjects by introducing advanced academic material in kindergarten—material that used to be taught in first, second, and even the third grades. Children are being pushed harder and harder to excel academically earlier and earlier. By the time children reach the second or third grade, many are either burned out on school or bored and didn't attend to the teaching of fundamental skills; therefore, they failed to learn many important fundamentals. Once fundamentals are not learned well, the child will fall further and further behind, making school even less pleasant. Failure to learn fundamentals, as stated earlier, is the main cause of learning disabilities, which often accompany attentional problems.

"Back to basics" can also mean treating all students as if they were going to college. Woe to the student who is vocationally inclined, because to them there is little available. All students are subsumed under curricula that are intended as preparation for admission to college. Course content has therefore become elitist and more and more academic. This philosophy adds to the decline of fun, hands-on activities. Because about 60 percent of high school graduates do not go to college, it appears that the needs of the majority are not being met.

Years ago public schools had track systems; there were separate tracks for college students and for students with more vocational interests. Is there any reason we can't return to such a system? If a student changes his or her mind, then accommodations for a switch can be provided. Under such a system the needs of the majority of students can be met. Academics can be blended into their course content. If more children's needs were being met, fewer of them would be bored, hate school work, and wind up being labeled as ADD-ADHD.

Vocational education can be continued at the community colleges, again with provisions for an academic switch should a student change his mind. (By the way, the starting salaries for many vocations are considerably higher than for many college majors.)

Politicians have also campaigned for systems of SOL (standards of learning) tests to maintain academic parity between the fifty states. In theory this seems like a good idea. Curricula can be designed to cover topics that are tested on the SOLs.

New York State has had a system such as this in the high schools called the Regents Exams. It has proved to be an excellent system. Unfortunately, in other states politicians have made teachers' and administrators' salaries, and even their job retention, dependent on the outcome of the SOL tests. This is forcing personnel to engage in frantic and increasingly dishonest behaviors. More and more children and teachers are reporting that courses are becoming boring reviews of test items from previous tests, and students memorize test answers rather than enjoy learning. Could this robotlike and bland form of teaching be contributing to kids not paying attention, being disruptive, and being labeled ADD-ADHD?

I don't blame the teachers. They are fighting for survival. Some teachers want to leave the profession because it is no longer fun, and the pressures have become intolerable. Teachers, administrators, and students appear to be excessively stressed by connecting job security with the results of these tests. This was not the case in New York, and I fail to understand the current overzealousness of the politicians. They, if left unchecked, will continue to disrupt the excellence of education.

Politics is also destroying the quality of many state college systems. I teach in a state college, and for the last twenty years I have witnessed a decline in the attitude and motivation of students. Many professors from neighboring state campuses, as well as my immediate colleagues, complain bitterly about having to tolerate unmotivated students who openly display a classroom attitude of "I couldn't care less." Many states are operating on a political belief that college education should be for everyone. Going to college is becoming as compulsory as attending the public schools.

College courses are supposed to be designed to take students to the highest levels of human thought. Either many students are not motivated or not qualified to go to such levels, or professors are being forced to water down the course content to levels that allow the weakest students to survive. I call this teaching to the lowest common denominator. Each year more and more students are entering colleges with ADD-ADHD diagnoses. Special conditions have to be provided for them, such as giving them more time to take tests, tape recording lectures, receive special tutoring, and so forth. If my premise is correct that these are mostly kids who hate school work, what are they doing in state-supported colleges? I love learning. I want my students to love in-depth learning and not the abridged, less-thought-provoking substitutions.

The political culprit in public higher education appears to be the funding system. State colleges are funded by the number of students enrolled in the sophomore, junior, and senior years, so the emphasis has increasingly been on student retention. The more students who are kept from flunking out of college, the more funds the college receives. College administrators are basing their academic policies on keeping retention as high as possible. Colleges are becoming production lines for mass-produced, mediocre products. Big business has now replaced quality as the operating philosophy of colleges and universities. Commitment to quality is rapidly disappearing.

Student evaluations of professors, upon which promotions and raises are based, add to the problem. High grades are often given to win the votes of students. Add these two elements together, and the result is what I call the *dumbing down of American higher education*. It would be a simple piece of research for me to videotape students during college classes. Their bored looks, their stares at the ceiling or the clock, their foot wiggling and pencil tapping could all be interpreted as ADD-ADHD symptoms. Do we give them all Ritalin to improve classroom conditions?

WHAT POLITICIANS CAN DO

With meaningful changes in policy both the politicians and the public can be winners. Students at state colleges should be considered to be on scholarships, because a significant percentage of their college expenses are supplemented by tax dollars. Why are taxpayers supporting the education of students who either don't care or who do not have the ability to learn? Politicians can win by *designating the size of each state institution*, which can be based on the statistics of the state's demographics. Some states already do this; many do not. Many have overbuilt the colleges and are desperate to fill all the seats and dorms. By designating size in overserved states and providing space for the better students, colleges can eliminate much of the expense throughout the state schools, including the number of professors, the number of support personnel, and the large, overstaffed and very expensive marketing departments. Admissions can be based on a combined formula of scholarship excellence and financial need.

Remedial services for marginal students, including ADD-ADHD students, can be offered less expensively at community colleges. Unfortunately, the Americans with Disabilities Act now includes ADD-ADHD students because of the lobbying of the parent group (funded by the makers of Ritalin) called CHADD (Children and Adults with Attention Deficit Disorders); excluding them from four-year campuses may be illegal. With this shift in financial configuration, huge savings can be passed on to voters as significant reductions in taxes—a real vote-getter.

PLEASE HELP PASS THE WORD

Now that you've completed this workbook, you have a wonderful and healthy child. You've discovered that he or she never had a disease, that he or she is IA-HM and not ADD-ADHD. You've learned that by using proper parenting skills, not dangerous drugs, you got your child to be well behaved, pay attention when required to, and perform well academically. Many parents don't know yet what you do. They believe that their child is diseased and that powerful chemicals are necessary to help him or her function.

Pass the word on. Tell your friends, your child's pediatrician, your family physician, all the teachers you know, and, most especially, the therapist, psychologist, or psychiatrist who has been giving you bad advice that there is a better way. Your child is living proof to others of what can be done with parenting, not drugs! You now know that Ritalin is not the answer. Please help by telling others.

AFTERWORD

There are two chores left I'd like your help with in my fight against drugging children and for advancing proper parenting as a better alternative. Complete the Behavior Rating Scale in Chapter Five and mail it to me (my address is in the chapter). I'd also like you to write a brief letter to me and share your experience with the Caregivers' Skills Program. Your identity and that of your child will be kept strictly confidential. Your story can help convince others that what you have learned is a better, more lasting, and healthier alternative to Ritalin and other drugs. I look forward to hearing from you.

RESOURCES FOR PARENTS

INSTITUTIONS

Center for Affirmative Parenting
John Rosemond, Director
PO Box 4124
Gastonia, NC 28054-0020
Phone: (704) 864-0851
E-mail: whrosemond@aol.com

International Center for the Study of Psychiatry and Psychology
Peter Breggin, Director
4628 Chestnut Street
Bethesda, MD 20814
Phone: (800) 595-2763
Fax: (970) 668-5030
E-mail: MERVISION@aol.com

PRACTICING THERAPISTS AVAILABLE FOR DRUG-FREE TREATMENT, PARENT TRAINING, AND PROFESSIONAL SEMINARS IN THE CAREGIVERS' SKILLS PROGRAM (CSP) FOR IA-HM (ADD-ADHD) CHILDREN (IN ALPHABETICAL ORDER BY STATE)

Kevin McCready, Ph.D., Clinical Director
San Joaquin Psychotherapy Center
Clovis, CA 93612
Phone: (559) 292-7572
Web site: www.medsfree.com

Ty Colbert, Ph.D.
PO Box 3907
Tustin, CA 92781
Phone: (714) 838-9771
E-mail: TYCO@aol.com

Robert Foltz, Psy.D.
Mailing address: 319 S. Western, Park Ridge, IL 60068
Office address: 100 S. Atkinson, Suite 203, Grayslake, IL 60030
Phone: (847) 295-8321 or (847) 245-6472
E-mail: bfoltz@allendale4kids.org

Peter C. Horsley, L.C.P.C.
9401 Nall, Suite 101
Prairie Village, KS 66207-2900
Phone: (913) 648-7010
Fax: (913) 341-9701
E-mail: phorsley@swbell.net

Charlotte Saji, L.C.P.C. and School Counselor
Common Sense Solutions, L.L.C.
43 Randolph Road #104
Silver Spring, MD 20904
Phone: Office (301) 622-9061; School (410) 880-5840

Lloyd Ross, Ph.D.
27 North Broad Street
Ridgewood, NJ 07450
Phone: (201) 445-0280
E-mail: hollij@WORLDNET.att.net

Michael C. Gibert, Psy.D., Founder-Director
It's About Childhood and Family, Inc.
3720 Welsh Church Road
Erieville, NY 13061
Phone: (315) 662-3627 or (315) 382-0541
E-mail: mgilbert@freside.scsd.k12.ny.us

Jessica E. Sicherman, Psy.D.
It's About Childhood and Family, Inc.
3720 Welsh Church Road
Erieville, NY 13061
Phone: (315) 662-3627

S. DuBose Ravenel, M.D.
Cornerstone Pediatrics
611 Lindsay Street
Suite 200-A
High Point, NC 27262
E-mail: Dbravenel@aol.com

Deborah Johnson, Ed.S., L.P.C., N.C.C.
569 Peavine Firetower Rd.
Crossville, TN 38571
Phone: (931) 456-2732
E-mail: dcuva@usit.net

REFERENCES

Amen, K. G., Paldi, J. H., & Thisted, R. A. (1993). Brain SPECT imagining. *Journal of the American Academy of Child and Adolescent Psychiatry, 32,* 1080–1081.

American Psychiatric Association. (1994). *Diagnostic and statistical manual of mental disorders* (4th ed.). Washington, DC: Author.

Arnold, L. E., Kleykamp, K., Votolato, N., & Gibson, R. A. (1994). Potential link between dietary intake of fatty acids and behavior: Pilot exploration of serum lipids in attention deficit hyperactivity disorder. *Journal of Child and Adolescent Psychopharmacology, 4,* 171–182.

Baldessarini, R. J. (1985). *Chemotherapy in psychiatry: Principles and practice.* Cambridge, MA: Harvard University Press.

Baldwin, S., & Anderson, R. (2000). The cult of methylphenidate: Clinical update. *Critical Public Health, 10,* 81–86.

Bandura, A. (1986). *Social foundations of thought and action: A social cognitive theory.* Upper Saddle River, N.J.: Prentice Hall.

Barkley, R. A. (1981). *Hyperactive children: A handbook for diagnosis and treatment.* New York: Guilford Press.

Barkley, R. A. (1993). *ADHD: What do we know?* New York: Guilford Press (Video).

Barkley, R. A. (1995). *Taking charge of ADHD: The complete authoritative guide for parents.* Nebraska: Boys Town Press.

Beck, A. T. (1991). Cognitive therapy. *American Psychologist, 46,* 368–375.

Bradley, C. (1937). The behavior of children receiving Benzedine. *American Journal of Psychiatry, 94,* 577–585.

Breggin, P. R. (1998). *Talking back to Ritalin: What doctors aren't telling you about stimulants for children*. Monroe, MA: Common Coverage Press.

Castellanos, F. X., et al. (1994). Quantitative morphology of the caudate nucleus in attention deficit hyperactivity disorder. *American Journal of Psychiatry, 151*, 1791–1796.

Comings, D. E., et al. (1991). The dopamine D2 receptor locus as a modifying gene in neuropsychiatric disorders. *Journal of the American Medical Association, 266*, 1793–1800.

Cook, E. H., Jr., Stein, M. A., & Leventhal, B. L. (1997). Family based association of attention-deficit/hyperactivity disorder and the dopamine transporter. In K. Blum & E. P. Noble (Eds.), *Handbook of Psychiatric Genetics* (pp. 297–310). Boca Raton, FL: CRC Press.

Davison, G. C., & Neale, J. M. (1978). *Abnormal psychology: An experimental clinical approach*. New York: Wiley.

DeGrandpre, R. J. (1999). *Ritalin nation: Rapid-fire culture and the transformation of human consciousness*. New York: W. W. Norton.

Ebaugh, F. G. (1923). *Neuropsychiatric sequelae* of acute epidemic Encephalitis in children. *American Journal of Disease in Children, 25*, 89–97.

Gallagher, M. (1989). *The abolition of marriage: How we destroy lasting love*. Washington, DC: Regency.

Gibson, W. (1957). *The miracle worker: A play for television*. New York: Knots.

Giedd, J. N., et al. (1994). Quantitative morphology of the corpus callosum in attention deficit hyperactivity disorder. *American Journal of Psychiatry, 151*, 665–669.

Greenblatt, J. M., Huffman, L. C., & Reiss, A. L. (1994). Folic acid in neurodevelopment and child psychiatry. *Progress in Neuropsychopharmacology and Biological Psychiatry, 18*, 647–660.

Halperin, J. M., et al. (1997). Serotonin, aggression and parental psychopathology in children with attention-deficit hyperactivity disorder. *Journal of the Academy of Child and Adolescent Psychiatry, 36*(10), 1391–1398.

Heilman, K. M., Voeller, K. K., & Nadeau, S. E. (1991). A possible pathophysiologic substrate of attention deficit hyperactivity disorder. *Journal of Child Neurology, 6*, S76–S81.

Hyman, I. (1999). *The case against spanking: How to discipline your child without hitting*. San Francisco: Jossey-Bass.

Joseph, J. (1999). The genetic theory of schizophrenia: A critical review. *Ethical Human Sciences and Services, 1*(12), 119–145.

Lahat, E., et al. (1995). BAEP studies in children with attention deficit disorder. *Developmental Medicine and Child Neurology, 37*, 119–123.

Larzelere, R. (1999). A debate held at the Conference of the National Foundation for Family Research and Education at Banff in Alberta, Canada, June.

Levy, F. (1991). The dopamine theory of attention deficit hyperactivity disorder. *Australian and New Zealand Journal of Psychiatry, 25*, 277–283.

Maxmen, J. S., & Ward, N. G. (1993). *Psychotropic drugs fast facts* (2nd ed.). New York: W. W. Norton.

McGee, J. P., & De Barnado, C. R. (1999). The classroom avenger. *The Forensic Examiner, 8*, 5–6.

National Institutes of Health. (1998). ADHD Consensus Conference, Bethesda, Maryland.

Odell, J. D., Warren, R. P., Warren, W. L., Burger, R. A., & Maciulis, A. (1997). Association of genes within the major histocompatibility complex with attention deficit hyperactivity disorder. *Neuropsychobiology, 35*(4), 181–186.

Peele, S. (1995). *The diseasing of America: How we allowed recovery zealots to convince us we are out of control.* San Francisco: Jossey-Bass.

Phelan, T. (1984). *1–2–3 magic! Training your preschoolers and preteens to do what you want.* Glen Ellyn, IL: Child Management.

Phelan, T. (1984). "1–2–3 magic! Training your preschoolers and preteens to do what you want." Glen Ellyn, IL: Child Management (Video).

Physicians Desk Reference. (2000). Oradell, NJ: Medical Economics.

Pizzi, W. J., Rode, E. C., & Barnhart, J. E. (1986). Methyphenidate and growth: Demonstration of a growth impairment and a growth-rebound phenomenon. *Developmental Pharmacology and Therapeutics, 9*, 361–368.

Ravenel, S. D. (1997). To spank or not to spank: That is the question. *The North Carolina Pediatrician, 7*(1), 1–3.

Samango-Sprouse, C. (1999). Frontal lobe development in childhood. In B. L. Miller & J. L. Cummings (Eds.), *The human frontal lobes: Functions and disorders. The science and practice of neuropsychology series* (pp. 584–603). New York: Guilford Press.

Sedvall, G. (1997). The current status of PET scanning with respect to schizophrenia. *Neuropsychopharmacology, 7*(1), 41–54.

Seligman, L. (1994). *DSM-IV: Diagnosis and treatment planning.* Alexandria, VA: American Counseling Association (Audio).

Stein, D. B. (1999). *Ritalin is not the answer: A drug-free, practical program for children diagnosed with ADD or ADHD.* San Francisco: Jossey-Bass.

Stein, D. B. (2000). Attention deficit hyperactivity disorder: Behavioral innovations offer medication or nonmedication prescription choices. In F. F. Edlich (Ed.), *Advances in Medicine.* Arlington, VA: ABI Professional Publications.

Stein, D. B., & Baldwin, S. (2000, Aug.). Toward an operational definition of disease, in psychology and psychiatry: Implications for diagnosis and treatment. *International Journal of Risk and Safety in Medicine*, pp. 65–84.

Still, G. F. (1902). The Coulstonian lectures on some abnormal physical conditions in children. *Lancet, 1*, 1008–1082.

Straus, A., & Lehtinen, L. W. (1947). *Psychopathology and education of the brain impaired child.* New York: Greene & Stratton.

Straus, M. (1999). A debate held at the conference of the National Foundation for Family Research and Education at Banff in Alberta, Canada.

Swanson, J. M., et al. (1993). Effect of stimulant medication on children with ADD: A review of reviews. *Exceptional Children, 60,* 154–161.

Valenstein, E. (1998). *Blaming the brain: The truth about drugs and mental health.* New York: Free Press.

Weiner, I. B. (1982). *Child and adolescent psychopathology.* New York: Wiley.

Witters, W., Venturelli, P., & Hanson, G. (1992). *Drugs and society* (3rd ed.). Boston: Jones & Bartlett.

Yax, L. K. (2000). *Marriage and divorce rates.* Washington, DC: U.S. Census Bureau.

Zametkin, A. J., et al. (1993). Cerebral glucose metabolism in adults with hyperactivity of childhood onset. *New England Journal of Medicine, 323,* 1361–1366.

THE AUTHOR

David B. Stein is a professor of psychology at Longwood College, a state college in central Virginia. He has an extensive list of research publications and professional presentations. His books include:

Ritalin Is Not the Answer: A Drug-Free, Practical Program for Children Diagnosed with ADD or ADHD

Unraveling the ADD/ADHD Fiasco: Successful Parenting Without Drugs

Controlling the Difficult Adolescent: The REST Program (Real Economy Program for Teens)

Affectionately known as Dr. Dave, Stein has won numerous honors and awards for his twenty-five years of devoted work in offering drug-free treatment and parenting alternatives for the most difficult and out-of-control children and teens. Listed in *Who's Who Among America's Teachers* for many years, he is a diplomate, the highest clinical rank in medicine and psychology, and was awarded outstanding teacher and scholar for 2000 at Longwood. His research on ADD-ADHD treatment was selected as one of the top ten presentations for media coverage at the 1997 American Psychological Association convention.

His book *Ritalin Is Not the Answer* was endorsed as required reading by all parents, educators, and doctors at the 2001 Ritalin Litigation Conference in New York. Since his work was featured in the recent text *Advances in Medicine*, pediatricians and family physicians are increasingly prescribing his books as an alternative to drugs and reporting excellent success. When asked to describe himself, he readily states, "My most important position is being dad to three wonderful children."

A highly sought after public speaker, Stein recently became a member of national columnist and writer John Rosemond's Affirmative Parenting team. He now answers readers' questions at the Affirmative Parenting Web site www.rosemond.com and will be a featured writer for Rosemond's new magazine, *Traditional Parent*. Information about Stein, his speaking schedule, and how to arrange speaking engagements can be made by contacting Mrs. Mary Dillon at 704–864-1012, ext. 11, or Dr. Stein at dstein@wc.edu.

INDEX